Raphael

Nothing Can Stop God from Reaching Us

A Dachau Diary by a Survivor

Edizioni Carmelitane

ROMA

Translated by: Hanneke Veerman
Edited by: William Harry, O. Carm.

ISBN: 978-88-7288-094-4
IT ISSN: 0394-7750

EDIZIONI CARMELITANE
Via Sforza Pallavicini, 10
00193 Roma, Italia
edizioni@ocarm.org
carmelites.info/edizioni

Finito di stampare nel mese di Luglio 2007
dalla Tip. Città Nuova

TABLE OF CONTENTS

CURRICULUM VITAE
OF BROTHER RAPHAEL TIJHUIS, O. CARM.
(1913 – 1981)

1913 October 10	Bernhard Tijhuis born in Rijssen, the Netherlands
1932	Enters the Carmelite Order in Boxmeer, the Netherlands, and receives "Raphael" as his religious name
1933	Makes profession in the monastery of Merkelbeek, the Netherlands
1933	Moves to the Carmelite monastery in Mainz, Germany
1940 July 25	Arrested by the Gestapo in the monastery, held in the prison of Mainz
1940 October 30	Court trial; Raphael is sentenced to 18 months in jail with three months to count as served
1940 November 8	Transferred to *Strafvollzugsanstalt Frankfurt-Preungesheim* to serve the remainder of his sentence
1942 January 31	Instead of being released, confined in the police station of Frankfurt
1942 February 5	Transported by train to Darmstadt, held at Gestapo headquarters
1942 March 12	On transport to Dachau, stopover in Würzburg

1942 March 13	Arrives at the Dachau concentration camp, admitted to *Zugangsblock*
1942 March 30	Enters Block 28, the "priest's barracks" for non-German clerics
1942 April 2	Meets Henny Zwaans, a Dutch Jesuit priest, in Block 28
1942 June 19	Encounters Titus Brandsma, a Dutch Carmelite priest, at the *Zugangsblock*
1942 June 29	Titus Brandsma joins Raphael in Block 28
1942 July 26	Titus Brandsma dies in the sick barracks after a lethal injection
1942 July 27	Henny Zwaans dies of dysentery
1942 November 19	Admitted to the "experimental ward" of the camp infirmary as a guinea pig for malaria experiments
1943 January 5	Transferred from the sick barracks to Block 26, the "priest's barracks" for German clergy
1945 April 29	Liberation of the Dachau camp by American Infantry troops
1945 May 20	Leaves Dachau, returns to the Netherlands
1945 May 25	Arrives at Rijssen, reunited with his parents. Starts to write about his five years of imprisonment
1946	Stays at the Carmelite monastery in Nijmegen, the Netherlands
1947	Transferred to Rome, works at the Carmelite *Collegio Sant' Alberto*, first as a porter, then as a librarian

1956	Witness in 's-Hertogenbosch, the Netherlands in the proceedings leading to the beatification of Titus Brandsma
1980	Returns to the Carmelite monastery in Mainz, Germany
1981 June 5	Raphael Tijhuis dies in Mainz; he does not survive his fifth heart attack

AN INTRODUCTION
TO BROTHER RAPHAEL TIJHUIS

Why would I write about the horrors of the concentration camp?" This is the question Brother Raphael Tijhuis asked himself in the summer of 1945. He had just begun to write about the five years he spent imprisoned in Germany— beginning with almost two years in three prisons, then more than three years in *Konzentrationslager Dachau*. "But we have to speak," he continued, "the dead must speak through us." He had no choice, this 31-year old Carmelite brother, but to testify in the name of all those who had died and given their lives. So, during the summer of 1945, just released from the camp, he wrote down his story while in his hometown Rijssen where he was trying to recover from five years of hunger and misery. It is a story that begins on July 25, 1940, when he was arrested in the sacristy of the Carmelite monastery in Mainz, and ends on May 20, 1945, the day he passed through the gates of the Dachau concentration camp to return to his homeland, on his way towards freedom.

To survive a concentration camp for more than three years means you are one of the stronger ones. Many can endure such an ordeal no longer than a few months. For some it is only a matter of weeks. Professor Titus Brandsma, a Carmelite priest, 61 years of age and confrere of Raphael, was in the camp for just 37 days. Then he died in the hell of Dachau, where he had arrived in June 1942, worn out, sick and exhausted after five months of imprisonment in Scheveningen and the transit camp of Amersfoort. During those 37 days, he was in Raphael's company as much as possible. Raphael was 28 years old at the time and by then had lived through his first three months in Dachau.

They were together for a few weeks only, but when Raphael was a witness in Titus Brandsma's beatification proceedings in 1956, many vivid memories came back to him. Once again he took up his pen to describe day by day how Titus Brandsma had "lived" in the camp. *I'm All Right* is the title of that story. It is a moving account of events that are almost beyond words. Yet Raphael managed to write about them with sensitivity and distance, so that in the horrendous and horrific misery of camp life, pieces of friendship, brotherhood, hope and trust in God in whose hands both felt secure, are lightened up.

All of Raphael's writings have been saved: in 1981, when Raphael died, his papers were handed over to the archives of the Dutch Carmelite Institute in Boxmeer. Twenty years later they turned up again. A Carmelite priest, Constant Dölle, was writing a spiritual biography on Titus Brandsma[1], by now beatified, the priest who was killed in Dachau in July 1942. Dölle puts Raphael's story of his days with Titus Brandsma in Dachau to good use; Dölle is able to form some notion about the last weeks of Titus.

During the final stage of the book I spent many hours with the author, as we worked on the last chapters, par-

---

[1] C. Dölle, *Encountering God in the Abyss: Titus Brandsma's Spiritual Journey*, Leuven, 2002.

ticularly the part about Dachau. Thus I got acquainted with the life of Titus Brandsma, the spirituality of the Carmelite Order and monastic life, a life almost unknown to me as a non-Catholic. I got to know Raphael as well. The archive files contain many hand-written and typed sheets, drawings and letters. Once you start reading, you step into a different time, a world that is not ours. This happened to me after I was given the files together with the request: "Would you have a look at it and see if you can make it into something?"

Dölle met Raphael a couple of times after the war, when the latter lived in Rome. The years in the concentration camp were never mentioned. As I read, while the numerous note-bloc sheets with the immaculate handwriting went through my hands, I began to understand why. "I no longer belong to the others or the others no longer belong to me," Raphael wrote, words that echo a loneliness that is forever and irreversible.

The inhuman can only be shared with fellow-sufferers. Who else is able to feel what you have gone through? There is the annual reunion of "Dachau priests." A picture from 1950 shows Raphael was not present. He was in Rome according to the notes. Serious-minded men in long black garbs, sitting in half a circle in the garden of the host: these were his friends. He knew them and they knew him.

"Maybe it was difficult to get close to you, and you also longed to join Titus." I read this sentence in a copy of a magazine from 1965, when someone from the KRO, the Dutch Catholic broadcasting company, interviewed you. The interview was occasioned by the possible beatification of Titus Brandsma. For the first time I saw your picture: a tall heavy man with a fleshy face, black-rimmed glasses common in those years. Nothing shows that once you were an emaciated frame, just skin and bones, dragging yourself along, not even capable of remembering the names of your two brothers. Laughing, you mentioned the day in 1947 when Archbishop Beran was ordained cardinal: "Of course, there was a reception with many dignitaries and a lot of purple. You know what I mean. There I stand, in the midst of all this, modestly dressed in my common friar's habit. Suddenly Cardinal Beran rushes towards me and embraces me. Everyone is really surprised that someone like the Cardinal allows himself to approach a Carmelite brother in this way, and that I simply call him 'Joseph'. But what can I say? In the camp we washed each other's backs and shared a plank bed …"

Such an anecdote demonstrates a talent for handling such situations with a humor that alters their meaning. In choosing a different, uncommon perspective, you become someone who watches without looking, who sees without judging from a pure point of view that for you God is real. No doubt these qualities saved your life during the indescribable years in the camp. At the right moment you made the right choice and stepped forward during roll call or you remained in hiding instead. You answered a Nazi or you suffered brutality in silence. Your actions were not always logical; you had both the insight and the intuition to act on the spur of the moment. "Beauty is action in contemplation," according to Cardinal Danneels in his Titus Brandsma lecture.[2] Your story shows again and again that imme-

---

[2] G. Danneels, *Honger naar spiritualiteit,* Nijmegen, 2000.

diate action holds such beauty. In the standard work on the clergymen of Dachau, which contains all the possible information about the more than 2700 priests and other clerics who were imprisoned in Dachau, Raphael is mentioned in particular: "With his humor he knows how to handle and overcome dangerous situations and is capable of brightening up the lives of many."[3]

In Dachau, your trust in God was a gift you received with both hands each and every day. With 300 to 400 clerics from different countries you shared one of the four *Stuben* in the barracks. Brotherhood was never lived more intensely than during those years. After liberation and back in the monastery, it must have been hard to be "just a brother" and accept hierarchical relationships that were very strict in those days. "I hope I will live long enough to be present at the beatification of Titus," you said in the interview in 1965. "After that, Titus may come and fetch me!"

It was not meant to be. Titus Brandsma was beatified in 1985; Raphael Tijhuis died in 1981, at 67 years of age, from a heart attack, the fifth one within two years. In his obituary he was commemorated as someone with a lot of friends from all over the world to whom he meant a lot, but also as a person who came back from the war as a psychically and physically damaged man. As years went by, it became more and more difficult to keep camp experiences at a distance. Raphael suffered from severe depressions and anxieties: he could burst into panic at the sight of a pedestrian crosswalk, because it reminded him of the black and

---

[3] E. Weiler, *Die geistlichen in Dachau*, Modling, 1971.

white striped uniform. It was as if the brutes of the old days seized him by the collar again. What happened to him was happening to many other survivors of concentration camps who suffered from symptoms of KZ (concentration camp) syndrome in later life.

To come to know more about Raphael than I now knew, I decided to get in touch with some of his relatives, nephews and nieces to whom Raphael was "Uncle Bernard".

Raphael was born Bernard Tijhuis on October 10, 1913 in Rijssen, a small town within easy reach of Almelo. In those years, Rijssen was a small community, Protestant in majority and sound in the faith. This led to the situation that apart from the Reformed Church and the Calvinist Church, a number of smaller denominations split off. The dividing lines made for sharp distinctions and to make sure that different groups did not run into each other, there was a strict division of who bought in which shops. Working life was typical for a small countryside town of that period. Laborers mainly worked in the Ter Horst jute mill. Rijssen included many farmers as well. Shopkeepers and tradesmen, the class to which Raphael's parents belonged, were predominantly Catholic. The Catholic enclave accounted for about ten percent of the inhabitants of Rijssen.

Raphael was the youngest in a family of three sons; Hendrik, the elder son, was followed by Gerard. The family lived at Wierdensestraat not far from Grotestraat, on the outskirts of the town center. The parents were plain hard-working people who wanted the best for their three sons. Mother Tijhuis was very much dedicated to her family; the father was more outgoing and loved to travel. He was the town's blacksmith and his smithy was behind the house. This was where he did all the work, like shoeing horses. Later on he also started an ironmonger's shop. When Raphael was in the forge, he saw his father welding, busy poking up the fire, forging the red-hot iron at the right moment. So, as a young boy, he knew already that such a moment exists and you should not let it slip. Many years later, in the concentration camp, he was able to recognize and use such moments.

The three sons all became craftsmen. The elder, Hendrik, was his father's successor in the smithy as well as in the shop. Gerard became a carpenter and started an ironmonger's shop too. Raphael was apprenticed to a housepainter. But in 1932, at the age of 19, he entered the monastery of the Carmelites in Boxmeer, and one year later he took vows in their monastery in Merkelbeek. After that he was transferred to the Carmelite monastery in Mainz that belonged to the Dutch Carmelite province at that time. He had been living in that monastery for over six years when the Gestapo came to take him away on July 25, 1940.

After the war, having recovered as much as possible physically, Raphael was sent to Rome; since he was still suffering the consequences of medical experiments he underwent in Dachau, the warm weather in Rome suited him better than the cold and humid climate of the Netherlands.

In Rome, where he lived for the next thirty-something years, he began to work as a porter at Sant' Alberto, the Carmelite's international college. He also started professional training as a librarian. Apart from that, he dedicated himself to the beatification of Titus Brandsma. One of his course-papers was a biography and bibliography of Titus, written in Italian, German and English (the supplemented bibliography was officially published in 1991).[4] Raphael had a natural talent for languages and he took a lot of pleasure in them as well. In the spring of 1960, an article on Titus Brandsma authored by him was published in the English quarterly *Aylesford Review*, the journal of the oldest English Carmelite monastery in Aylesford.[5]

His family back in the Netherlands did not see much of him anymore: once every three years he would return home for a short vacation, staying in the family home which Hendrik had moved into. His nephews and nieces hung upon his every word when he would start telling stories about faraway Italy and how he had travelled for three days to get to the Netherlands. Raphael was a sociable person and he loved to talk a lot. He was also a fanatical stamp collector. Shoeboxes filled with stamps were piled up in his room in the monastery, and his collection of special stamps, in particular those of the Vatican, was so extraordinary that it had been put on exhibition more than once.

His nephews told me how impressed they used to be by the high-ranking people that came to visit, arriving by chauffeur-driven cars, because of Raphael's stamp collection; the people that came around during Raphael's stay were not seen that often in Rijssen. Also the celebration in honor of the 25th anniversary of his profession remained in their memories as a huge event.

---

[4] *Titus Brandsma O. Carm (1881-1942): A Bibliography of His Printed Writings* compiled by Rafael Tijhuis O. Carm; revised and translated by Joachim Smet O. Carm, Roma ,1991.

[5] R. Tijhuis, "Father Titus Brandsma," *Aylesford Review*, vol 3, no. 1 (1960).

As Raphael got older, other images came forward: a lonely man, living a more or less isolated and remote life in Rome and, at the end of his life, in Mainz, back in the monastery where he had been arrested in 1940.

During his rare visits to the Netherlands, Raphael was always busy; busy visiting people he had met in Rome, fellow survivors of Dachau and the people he was acquainted with through his stamp collection. He also spent a lot of time taking photographs and drawing. Drawing was what he loved to do, and his sketches were like his stories: simple but accurate pictures of what he saw and experienced. Take for instance the drawings of his cell in the prison in Mainz, the camp street in Dachau, the chapel, the crematorium and the revolting punishments by the Nazis. However, he also drew a picture of the family home of the wife of one of his cousins, a Saxon farm at Grotestraat. His drawings were exhibited in Rijssen many years after the war.

During his life abroad he stayed in contact with his elder brother Hendrik. Hendrik was also the one who kept up the correspondence that was granted to the prisoners in Dachau, sometime in 1943. In the files, I found some neatly typed letters with short messages about the family weal and woe and the forthcoming engagement of Hendrik, who expressed his hopes that Raphael would be able to attend the wedding. At the bottom were two handwritten lines. One from his father, "Dear Bernard, my beloved son, happy Christmas and a blessed 1944, hope to see you soon, Father." Then from his mother, putting all the love and worry she felt for her son, who had such a hard time so far away, in one moving sentence, "Hello Bernard, I do hope I will see you back again very soon."

So many things the parents had to endure! At the
end of the summer of 1942, they received the sad message of their son's death. What had happened? The
message about the death of Titus Brandsma had
reached Rijssen, where, in the dialect of that region,
one spoke of "Titoes' death." As news spread mainly
from mouth to mouth, this soon changed into "the
death of Tiehoes," as the common name of "Tijhuis" is
pronounced there. It took some weeks before the mis-
understanding was cleared up.

His parents meant a lot to Raphael. After the first
horrible year in Dachau when he had more or less
adapted to the miserable circumstances, he became
homesick—homesick for his parents and his hometown. When he was finally able to leave Dachau on
May 20, 1945, Rijssen was the destination of his journey. There, in his family home, he started to write. It
was his way to take up the thread of his life again.

In the mid-fifties, Raphael started to write about his
experiences in Dachau again; the detailed account of
the six weeks Titus Brandsma spent in Dachau takes
over fifty pages. It is a report in which Raphael is the
observer in the background and the spotlight is on the
figure of Titus. He also worked on a German language
version of the story of Father Othmarus Lips, a Dutch
priest who survived Dachau as well.[6] In the files, I
came upon this thematically ordered report of 90
pages. Raphael added his own experiences to Father

---

[6] P. Othmarus, OFM Cap., *Van pij en boevenpak*, 's-Hertogen-
bosch, 1946.

Othmarus' subjects, such as an impressive, detailed eyewitness account of the liberation of the camp. It reads as if we were in the midst of it, together with Raphael.

I have used both above-mentioned documents to complete the chronological story Raphael wrote in Rijssen immediately after his return from Dachau in 1945. This account turned out to be incomplete: a number of pages are missing. It ends somewhere in 1944, when Dachau starts to be flooded with evacuees from other concentration camps. In the above-mentioned German language version, however, he describes in great detail the unimaginable atrocity of the final months when typhus breaks out in the overpopulated camp. I have translated and included this part of Raphael's notes in German, which, together with his eyewitness account of the liberation of the camp, completes the story Raphael wrote in Rijssen in 1945.

For some detailed information about what happened shortly after the liberation of the camp and about the repatriation of the Dutch prisoners, I used copies of *De stem der lage landen*, ("Voices of the Lowlands"), the official newspaper of the Dutch colony in Dachau. This newspaper was set up by some Dutch camp inmates, among them the writer Ed Hoornik, right after the liberation of the camp. There were ten or more editions of this newspaper in Raphael's files.

I slightly modernised the style of Raphael's writing and made some corrections as well: since he spent so many years in Germany, the construction of his sentences in Dutch was "Germanized" now and then. I also had to make choices, and so parts of the manuscript were left out. For instance, the book does not cover each time Raphael is admitted to the camp hospital. I also chose to leave out the very detailed description of the camp itself and much of the account of his first weeks in the admission block where one was trained and drilled to become a "model prisoner." Their inclusion would have led to a book twice as thick.

However, the parts where Raphael tells about the way he felt supported by his faith and reflected on the meaning of his suffering in the German prisons and Dachau and the Passion of Christ are included almost without exception. This also goes for passages that picture the religious life of the priests in the "Priest Barracks" and the way they lived in this largest of all priest-communities. In addition, I have chosen those parts that tell us about the "normal" daily life in the prisons and the camp, and how Raphael coped with all this; here one can see a relativization and humor that, in my opinion, are essential to a religious perspective on life. Above all, the report is a personal, yet historical document that focuses on the life, experiences and observations of a young religious who, supported by his faith, managed to survive in indescribable and inhuman circumstances.

The parts in italics are text inserted to keep the story together. Sometimes I have summarized and rewritten parts of the original text that were left out, sometimes the italic parts contain a preview of what is going to happen or a commentary or an *intermezzo* in which factual information, always from original source material, helps to make the story of Raphael clearer. Some italicized texts, inserted at the right places, prepare the reader for the meeting between Raphael and his fellow Carmelite Titus Brandsma in Dachau. The episode that starts with the arrival of Titus Brandsma in Dachau and ends with his death needs special mention. Although it covers a period of only six weeks, the archive files contained an elaborate report of that period. When Raphael was heard as a witness in the official beatification proceedings of Titus Brandsma in 1956, he decided to write a lively and detailed description of what happened during those weeks. Thus we are able to follow Titus from the moment he entered the camp through the gate, stayed in the admission block, was assigned to a labor *Kommando*, had to endure humiliations and maltreatments, associated with Polish Carmelite priests in prayer and celebration, till the day that Raphael took him to the sick barracks. There he died within a week after the administering of a lethal injection. Raphael turned out to be a practical, caring confrere, who looked after Titus, badly debilitated and fairly clumsy. Titus was having a very hard time and lived his last days in sheer agony and torment. Although this particular story, *I Am All Right*, was written in the second half of the fifties – at least ten years after the chronological account of 1945 – it fits in very well, especially because of the vivid style and the fullness of details. In following Titus Brandsma from day to day, we get a clear picture of events that took place in the summer of 1942, the worst year for the imprisoned priests in Dachau. In that year alone, 900 priests, for the most part Polish, died from hunger and exhaustion.

The reader who has already taken notice of the extraordinary life of Titus Brandsma, will be moved by the convincing way he lived his last weeks. Others will read this episode as an example of lived brotherhood that renders meaning and brings light into an abyss of darkness.

Going through the documents that Raphael left behind, all sorts of questions crossed my mind, questions
I had already asked myself some twenty years before
when I started reading holocaust literature and the testimonies of survivors of concentration camps. "How is
it possible to survive such an ordeal? What keeps people going? Why do they choose to go on instead of giving up? How can they find meaning in life in a concentration camp? What is the meaning of such an existence?" I read about the way people drew on the incredible support and strength of their faith, how
people would find each other across all social classes,
over the dividing walls of churches and religious com-
munities, which seemed to be insurmountable obsta-
cles in normal daily life. However, there were also
many in the camp who lost their faith, called God to
account for the hell they found themselves in, and
turned away from Him in the deep silence. What
struck me the most were the stories of people for
whom church and religion had not played a main part,
but whose faith, tested in the camps and prisons, impressed me as sincere, authentic, plain, and pure.

It is the same kind of simple purity that strikes me in
the stories Raphael has put on paper. Inside the concentration camp, life is reduced to what it is. Raphael
writes: "After I lost everything that connected me with
my previous life– my belongings, my clothes, my hair,
my name– I felt my bonds with God becoming closer
and closer." Amid all the misery, through everything,
his faith is the pure and only source of his life. He does
not mention it all the time and in those words. However, the invisible presence of God can be found on
each page: in Raphael's optimism, in his acceptance of

what was, when he described a sunset, in his humor, in his suffering, and in his hope. His practical mind seemed to be inextricably connected with God's voice that always succeeded in reaching him, even when he was living in the deepest darkness. In his words, one could hear a simplicity and singleness that echoes a certainty that strikes us now as strange and almost childish.

Raphael lived the consequences of his faith while his own safety was at stake. The Nazis offered him a safe hiding place during the remaining time of the war; when he was in the last of three prisons, he got the opportunity to escape transportation to Dachau, only if he promised to renounce his faith by handing in his habit. However Raphael's freedom flowed from a humble service to God. In this he found the strength to persevere despite all the pain and the risk, even if he was to pay for it with his life. The same was true for the hundreds of priests who were imprisoned in Dachau and suffered tremendously from the hatred of religion on the part of the SS and the Communist guards. The bodies of the priests could be disposed of. The souls of the priests, however, were forever out of reach of the barbarian methods of the Nazi annihilation machine that sought a total devaluation of Christianity and the Christian faith.

Raphael's trust and faith in God who is the source and meaning of all that is alive, and his willingness to sacrifice his life were the reasons that he cannot but write in the name of all those who stayed behind in Dachau. His words contained the inheritance of hundreds of priests who were killed in Dachau, brothers with whom he shared the barracks for more than three years, fellow victims of medical experiments, companions in the same work gang. Their legacy to us is not the horror of their deaths, but the strength of their faith. Bergman (1997) stated that spiritual strength is unable to change anything when confronted with a power that kills human freedom and dignity.[7] Yet when one reacts with transcendental strength and a perspective of love, it can give meaning to circumstances and suffering.

In Raphael, we find someone with a clear view, attentive look and accurate pen that show us what is human, but also someone who makes us into a witness of God's tangibility. His eyes not only behold the absurdity and cruelty of the concentration camp, but see details, small events and incidents in his daily life as well as that of other camp inmates. In this way, he is more accessible to us and we sympathize with him, for instance, during his stay in the experimental block as a malaria guinea pig and during the last days before and during the liberation of the camp by American troops.

In times when technology suggests the technological ability of life, and efficacy, functionality, and economic laws have become guidelines for our actions, Raphael's story about his camp experiences and the priests of Dachau comes as a testimony of trust and hope. "The dead have to speak through us," are words Raphael uses in the introduction to his story. In writing, he tried to build a bridge to other people, people he no longer belonged to, so he said. No doubt, there are other testimonies still hidden in boxes and drawers,

---

[7] S. Bergman (ed.), *Martyrs: Contemporary Writers on Modern Lives of Faith*, San Francisco, 1996.

not yet rescued from oblivion, but written down with the same intention—to let the world know what happened and in honor of all those who opposed a great evil.

Each commemoration of those who died deliberately and conquered meaning through the loss of their lives, serves to honor the remembrance of those who were crushed *without* having had the choice. This is why I worked on the writings of Raphael; this is also why testimonies of survivors will always be worthwhile reading.

Nijmegen, Spring 2002

Hanneke Veerman

SOME GENERAL INTRODUCTORY REMARKS BY RAPHAEL TIJHUIS

So many people have asked questions about what life was like in the various prisons and the concentration camp in Germany, questions that are often impossible or at least difficult to answer. For a long time I have thought about whether I would write about Dachau or keep silent. Why talk about it? People would not be able to understand the experience at all; I no longer belong to the others and other people no longer belong to me. Why tell all about it? But we must speak up. Those who died are demanding that we speak and they are speaking through us. In their name I want to tell about Dachau, about the five years I was a prisoner in Germany, as well as in the name of professor Titus Brandsma, my dear friend, fellow prisoner and confrere. As long as I live, I will remember the last time I saw him when I took him to the *Revier*, the camp hospital. With a "see you again soon!" he said goodbye, completely exhausted but cheerful as always.

Although it is extremely difficult to give an objective account of what happened to me in those five years, I will nevertheless try to tell it as it was, so that the reader gets more or less an idea of what a concentration camp is like. Things happened that are beyond any description or fantasy; this does not mean, however, that every prisoner went through such barbarities. To avoid any exaggerating, the best I can do is to write about my own experiences. Thus I can stand by everything that is to be read in this report. I shall therefore confine myself to the

sober truth. I hope you will not blame me for not repre-
senting the facts in glowing official terms: a bird is
known by its note and a man by his words.

In reverence we look up to those who have preceded
us, the many from our own rows and all the other
thousands and thousands of all ranks and classes and
nationalities. Only now am I beginning to realise how
many different perils we have been exposed to.

Our deceased comrades must have surely been our
intercessors in Heaven. Many, many people back in
our homelands prayed for us; this is what all the letters
we were so privileged to receive tell us. Many of them
had to bear a heavy cross on their own shoulders, and
yet they never forgot us, the prisoners in Dachau. The
numerous parcels we received in Dachau prove that.
Without these supplies, none of us would have seen his
beloved ones again.

To us, "survivors of Dachau," the experience has not
been in vain. However horrific and horrible it may have
been, I would not want it out of my life. I could not
even live without it! Deep inside me, maybe more than
on the outside, it has left a huge impression on my life.
One learned to appreciate people and things much more
than before, although that is not the most important
thing. To have been in Dachau does not mean a lot. To
have found the way to deepen one's inner life and to be
a Christian means so much more. This would mean vic-
tory over the shadow of evil and the devilish forces of
the dark, which we encountered there. So many people
burst out in rage as soon as they hear anything about
concentration camps. All they want is revenge and the
only thing they do is resent everything that is German.
No matter how much we suffered under the yoke of the

Nazis, let us forgive; it is not our job to place blame. Others will take care of that.

When I consider my time in the concentration camp and the three prisons in the light of faith, not a single sparkle of hatred or any feeling of revenge enters my heart. To a Christian, one thing has to be clear: above and beyond the feeling of human retaliation stands the law of love. I would strain the Lord's Prayer, I would betray being a Christian if I would not practice love of neighbor and forgiveness to all, without regard to political affiliation, religion or nationality, especially right now after everything that has happened.

To be free is a thought that appears like a bad dream to someone who did not know freedom for five years and is enjoying it again now. But that freedom is real, and we cannot do anything better than to thank the good Lord for His great treasure of grace that helped us so much to conquer and survive all the difficulties, perils, hunger, and diseases.

The holy Archangel Raphael, my patron saint, led me alongside many dangerous roads; St. Anthony was a mighty helper to me and, not in the least, the Blessed Virgin Mary, Our Lady of Mount Carmel, who reached out her sheltering hand towards me. Without her powerful intercession and mediation with her divine Son, life would have been hell, unbearable for one without trust in God.

May God and our Heavenly Mother bless all who have supported us so vigorously, be it in the spiritual or in the temporal domain.

Rijssen, Assumption of the Holy Virgin Mary, 15th of August 1945.

FROM MONASTIC CELL
TO PRISON CELL

Raphael, the Gestapo is here to see you." With these nervous words, Brother Andreas comes rushing into the sacristy of our monastery in Mainz. It is nine twenty-five in the morning on Thursday, July 25, 1940. Date, day and even the exact time of the message would stick in my memory for a long time. I say, "Gestapo? What on earth could they want from me?" It is a question Andreas is not able to answer either. The Father Prior, who is about to get dressed to celebrate Mass, turns towards me and says, "What is the matter, Raphael? What are they here for?" I tell him I have not the faintest notion of what is going on, and that I might as well go and see what they want.

Two men are waiting for me in the parlor and they receive me with a "Heil Hitler" that I ignore. They ask me if I am Brother Raphael, at the same time making clear that they want to search my room. Although I know perfectly well with whom I am dealing, I tell them "First of all, I would like to know who is honoring me with a visit." As an answer one of them, probably the chief officer, shows me a badge that is hidden under his coat.

What else could I do than take them to my room? I tell them I will lead the way. They follow me and once we have arrived, their first question is if I carry on a foreign correspondence. I explain that, as a foreigner, I do have a regular exchange of letters with people in the Netherlands. Yes, they knew that all right! Both of them start to fumble among my letters and books but fail to find anything that suits them. After a thorough inspection of everything in my room, they ask me if know where to find Kaizerstraße, number 92 to be more precise. Their final question is if I am ready to join them. Outside they allow me to go ahead a few steps, so I do not have to walk next to them.

At the Gestapo headquarters at Kaizerstraße a picture of a letter is shown to me together with the question, if it is a letter of mine. I tell them it is indeed a copy of one of my letters. "Very well," but why did I not write my name on the envelope? I can only answer that it must have been a minor forgetfulness, and had not in any way been omitted for an ulterior motive. In his opinion, however, excuses will not bring me very far here, only confessing will. Yet a confession is out of the question, since I am not aware of any crime. In that case, I "might as well sit and wait until I know why I did not put my name as a sender on the envelope!" So I have waited five years, 58 months to be precise, and still I do not know, not even now!

Next, he inquires about some passages in the letter and what I had meant to say there. One line in particular is pointed out (it was a letter dated January 5, 1940, so before the war had even begun): "As a favor I will stamp this letter with the latest stamp, issued recently. I could not buy the complete issue, however, because it is too expensive for me." Now the Gestapo man claims that by using the words "too expensive," I am accusing the German Post Office of usury! It takes a great deal of talking before he believes that I never meant to say that, but the complete series was simply too expensive for me because of the additional charge. He also takes offense at one line out of a letter to the prior of the Carmelite monastery in Aalsmeer. "In case you are ever in need of a couple of bells, you may well have ours, since we are hardly ever allowed to ring them." This is considered to be a major crime as well. In those days, rumors were going around that church bells had to be handed in for purposes of war. That is why I wrote that line, not realizing that one day it would be held against me.

Eventually, the accusation concerns three letters – all dated before the war! – that Raphael had sent to his confreres in the Netherlands on the occasion of a birthday or saint's feast day. Sentences about stamps and daily life in the monastery are labelled as signs of opposition against the German Reich, the German nation and her leaders. After signing, all papers are put in a file. On the cover Raphael reads a word that he does not know from experience yet: "custody."

It is eleven-thirty by now and I am beginning to get tired of this. It is time to call it a day. After the Gestapo man has drawn up an impressive record, I think I can now go home. However, these things apparently take time and instead of saying goodbye and putting an interesting morning to an end, my "friend" takes me to Klarastraße, where the police station is located. They make me empty my pockets and I am clamped under lock and key. A moment later, a policeman appears and asks me if I have had dinner yet. After an answer in the negative from my side, it does not take long for the man to appear in the doorway once again, this time with a bowl of some traditional German potato salad and a piece of liver-sausage. It makes an impression that would not give an edge to a person's appetite (later in Dachau I would have simply loved it) and after having tasted a bit, I make a cross and leave the rest for what it is.

After a while, the police officer returns to fetch the bowl. He smiles, saying I was not a real crook yet, because instead of returning food, a criminal would have asked for more! His conclusion is that I am not a big eater at all. I have absolutely no intention to become one, I tell him; something he can understand perfectly well. We have a chat for a while and he expresses his hope that from now on there will be no further contact between me and the Gestapo.

By four o'clock, the Gestapo man from that morning comes to fetch me, this time to take me to Friedrichstraße, to the courtyard. Again, at first my particulars are registered in the same way as had happened at the Gestapo early that morning and at the police station in the afternoon. After a couple of irrelevant questions, a corpulent clerk reads out the notes in a bawling voice, as if he had to be heard outside the building. The examining judge leaves the room pointing to some chairs, inviting me to take a seat. After barely a second, the Gestapo man shouts at me that the invitation to sit was not meant for me but only for him. I stand up, not even listening to the rest of his shouting, as the door opens again and the judge enters. The first thing he tells me is to take a seat. "Do sit down. You do not have to stand." Thanking him, I look the Gestapo man straight in the face, giving him a bland nod that makes him turn deep red with pent-up rage.

After a few more formalities we can go. I am absolutely convinced by now that at least for today it is over, and as soon as we are outside I turn left in the direction of the monastery. "Hello, where are you off to?" he calls after me. I say, "Home." "Oh, one moment," and he takes me by the arm and leads me towards a gate across the street, where he rings the bell. After the iron door has opened, he steers me inside, saying just one word: *Zugang*. This is where the Gestapo man leaves me; his work is done.

Inside, I am told that I just have to go on as far as the end of the hall and that someone will be waiting for me there. As if by itself, a door swings open, and again I find myself in a long, wide hallway with many doors in deep alcoves. At the end I can see a group of prisoners at work and, deep in thought, I take a few steps in their direction. Suddenly a guard pops up in front of me, greeting me with a friendly *Grüß Gott*. He asks me if I am visiting someone or if I come as a "guest." Laughing, I tell him I cannot answer that question either way. "Oh well, in that case you must be a guest. Come with me, please." He takes me into a small office where a very unfriendly man shouts at me, "*Stramm zu stehen*." After a lot of bother, he orders to lock me up in the last cell on the first floor. Together with the guard, I walk in the direction of what will be my new home. At the corner of the long corridor my guard appears to be in a rush, for he gives me a punch in the back. "Hurry up. From now on you are a prisoner."

Cell 64 is to become my home, the door flings open with a pull, a young man jumps up and runs out and I am pushed inside. The door closes with a swing, and I find myself quite alone with the four bare walls of a prison cell. Four white chalked walls, but so different from the walls in my cloister cell that is filled with an atmosphere of peace and happiness. Everything here gives the impression of desolation and forlornness. I take a look around, but there is not much to see in my new "home" really. Beneath the window opposite the door is a rough white-sanded wooden table with a simple chair. In one corner a small locker hangs on the wall, containing an unappetizing mug that serves both dinner and coffee. There is only a spoon and a knife, sometimes taken away in the evening to prevent suicide attempts. When you stand underneath the barred windowpane and look in the direction of the door, you can see a bed fixed on the wall at the right hand side; in fact, it is not much more than a broad shelf. Behind the bed is the indispensable water closet, a barrel with a seat, better known among prisoners as "the throne" or "little throne." Between bed and throne stands an iron tripod that serves as washing-stand together with a badly battered enamel bowl and a ewer or water jug or whatever you may call it. Further, I see an old dustpan and a brush that can hardly claim to be the owner of one single hair. The heavy iron cell door has a small hole, the so-called spy-hole, through which it is possible to look from the hall into the cell unnoticed by its inhabitant. In the corner next to the door is a small radiator; only the guard can regulate its temperature. On the floor is linoleum, so it could look rather nice. For the rest, there is not much to see except for a small sliver of blue sky behind the barred window. In these surroundings, where no one keeps you company apart from an army of vermin, I spend the first fourteen weeks of my imprisonment.

Meanwhile, night is closing in and tired as I am, I lie down. Despite the stuffy atmosphere in the cell, I fall asleep almost straight away. Early in the morning at six, shouting voices wake me up. "*Kubel heraus.*" The door is opened, the toilet cleaned and fresh water brought in. Everything happens fast and then the door closes with a slam. A while later, coffee and a lump of bread are brought around with a lot of noise. In strong language, which I would rather not repeat here, I am yelled at to clean the cell. "The floor looks like a threshing-floor!" I brush as good as I can and with some effort I manage to get some "*Ordnung*" in my home; it is impossible to get rid of so much dirt in one time. For a change, I know of nothing better than to say my prayers, since I have not started my office yet. Here, in the solitude of a prison cell, I have learned to pray and appreciate it more than ever, for "need is the mother of prayer," to paraphrase the well-known adage.

Days last for ages and nights creep by slowly while I sit here without work, a visit from my fellow Carmelites or any distraction. Now, praying becomes my sole comfort and consolation. A person without trust in God would certainly go crazy in such a cramped space—six paces to and fro, nothing more. Yet, how I longed to be back here later when I was in Dachau. I would have crawled on my knees all the way back! How easy it is to meditate now, nothing around me disturbs my thinking of the greatest Prisoner and Sufferer of all times, our Lord and Savior himself. When on Sundays the other prisoners have permission to go to the chapel to attend Mass, my door remains locked; there is a sign at my door saying "No visitors allowed, not even the chaplain."

One day after the other goes by. To have something to do and to break through monotony, Raphael asks for work. And work is what he gets!

One Saturday afternoon the door of my cell swings open and two prisoners enter with huge piles of paper on their shoulders. Within moments my cell is filled in such a way that I can hardly turn around anymore. "So, there is your work and you better start with it now," I am told by the guard. "What am I supposed to do with all this?" I ask. "Well, that is obvious— making paper bags and as quick as you can!" is his grumpy reply. I ask for a demonstration to start with, since I have not done anything like this before. "Now what?" he shouts at me. "Your sort is good for noth- ing, not even making paper bags, let alone something else." Raving and raging, he shows me how to make a bag. In no time, a second one is done. Then he tells me to hurry up. "On Monday everything has to be done," are his last words. While leaving my cell, he threatens me in various ways, in case the work is not ready on Monday morning.

The intention is to make me work on Sunday, and even if I had been experienced in this line of business, I would have failed to complete the work considering the large stock he gave me. With little knowledge in this new "trade" I make a start, glad to have some dis- traction at last. The first ones take a while, but slowly it gets better and after a few hours I have "broken" some 40 or 50, to use the technical term. I am convinced I have achieved something already and I decide to call it a day. I can spend the rest of the time in quiet prayer. It is Saturday night by now. The beautiful heavy bells of the nearby Christchurch are chiming in Sunday and I even manage to catch the sound of our own bells re- sounding over the roofs of the town. I sink in a mood of melancholy and nostalgia when I think of the usual Saturday night procession that takes place right now in our Carmel, in honor of Our Blessed Mother, and also of the *Salve Regina*, the beautiful *Magnificat* and the long series of invocations of the litany of Our Lady by clear voices of the children. No wonder I completely lose my will for making paper bags at such reminiscences!

I kneel down and pray to Mary for help. She will be my strength in these dark days and the many more to come. "Holy Mary, Mother of Mount Carmel, pray for us!" Then it is as if my cell turns into Heaven. The atmosphere of sadness is gone to make room for contentment and complete surrender to God's holy will. No threatening by any guard can scare me. Nobody is able to take away my peace. Sunday is the day for prayer and not for "breaking" bags!

Rather early in the morning on Monday, the guard comes to fetch the results of my Sunday labor. Some prisoners take the bags that are ready, but it does not take long for the guard to return, pale with anger, scolding and raging because... my work is absolute rubbish. He yells at me, accusing me of large-scale sabotage, and all the material is removed from my cell as a punishment. What else can I do but take my rosary again. That suits me so much better!

The next day I try to get something to read. A fellow-prisoner in charge of the library has promised to help me. It takes quite a while before the guard answers my request and returns with two "nice" books. He has picked them himself, so he says— *Mein Kampf* and another beauty, *Speeches by Goebbels*! I put them away on top of my locker without giving them any further notice.

So there I am on the rocks again. After a couple of days the guard brings one more book. "Now I have something nice for you. I could not do much better." I take it and after some browsing I see immediately what he is trying this time. Never have my eyes seen a book with such a filthy content, so downright low and mean. In fact, the title *Holy Fire* said it all. That one ends on top of the locker as well, and I am not asking for books anymore.

The first Sundays as a prisoner are quite painful, because I am excluded from Sunday Mass that is celebrated by the prison chaplain. Never in my life had this happened and so I sit under lock and key and listen from a distance to the rest of the prisoners singing High Mass in the chapel right across from my cell, while I can half understand the chaplain's sermon.

In the meantime, Father Prior has succeeded in getting me a lawyer and the latter manages to get permission for me to attend Mass. It does not take long either before the first food parcel from the monastery is delivered. From now on there is regular contact with the monastery. My lawyer has arranged a permit to visit me every week and talk with me without a guard being present. The letters he brings from the monastery have to be censored first, so they reach me a couple of days later. The same goes for the newspaper. Both letters and newspaper are thrown into my cell in such a way that the papers go everywhere, while the guard says things like: "Let's see what the Holy Ghost has brought us today!" I decide it is about time to teach him a lesson, and within a week an opportunity arises. On Thursday, when he throws a copy of the *Catholic Illustration* inside again while reciting some biblical text, I say to him: "You have been studying the Scripture devotedly, I must say." "How come?" is his surprised reaction. I tell him what the Scripture says: "First find the Kingdom of God and everything else will fall into place." Never again is anything, be it book or newspaper, ever thrown into my cell. He had understood and since that day he hands them to me personally.

Sunday after Mass finds us in the exercise yard. When everyone else is outside, I am the last one to join the group. This is because I am still wearing my habit and anyone walking behind me would have difficulties in keeping step with me. For keeping in step painstakingly is very important, and as the last one in the row, I do not disturb anyone, since my "left-right" is certainly not military enough. But halfway, when the order is given to turn round, I walk in front and everyone else has to fit in with my steps. Within a minute, all are out of step. A regular mess it is! Such a walk in the courtyard of the prison, enclosed by four-story buildings on all four sides, lasts about half an hour. A piece of blue sky is all you can see; one can hear the noise of the city. That is all there is to learn from the outside world.

Every Thursday morning at nine-thirty I think, "Thank God, another week has gone by." Each 25th of the month means another month is over. I have figured out exactly what I am going to do the moment I am released. Yet days and weeks pass by without any of these small illusions being realized. I keep waiting and waiting. If I have to be here much longer, I will languish like a flower with no sunlight. I am worrying myself to death and sleepless nights give plenty of time to brood even more.

For my lawyer who visits me weekly it is obvious that I am deteriorating and getting more and more depressed. He demands my instant release because of poor health conditions and it does not take long before things get moving. My case will come up for trial as

soon as possible. On October 24th, my Saint's day, I receive the written *Anklage*, in which October 30th is
scheduled as the day that the session of the court will
take place.

*That week Raphael prays even more for God's mercy in
the hope that he is allowed to return to the monastery
soon. However, it is not meant to be. The court takes
place, but Raphael is not released. Instead, together with
other prisoners he is put on a transport to Preungesheim
near Frankfurt am Main.*

October 30th is court day, the session starts at 9 o'-
clock. A guard brings me into the courtroom, where I
have to take my place in the dock as a "major criminal." After some time the judge appears with his two
assistants, followed by the *General-Staatsanwalt*. The
judge is an older, grey-haired gentleman wearing horn-
rimmed spectacles on the tip of his nose. Besides that,
he is as deaf as a post. Whether one speaks in a loud
voice or even shouts, he does not hear a word. This becomes obvious when I have to approach the main table
and he asks me for how long I have been in Mainz. In
response to my answer "six years," he says, "Well, well,
four years already?"

After a few questions by the judge, the *General-
Staatsanwalt* starts his speech, sparkling with hate
and resentment against churches and cloisters, explaining my letters in a roaring voice as an instigation
against the Third Reich. Then my lawyer starts his
plea. As a excellent speaker and a good counsel for
the defense of everything I am accused of, he speaks
for three quarters of an hour, making both the judge
and the *Staatsanwalt* rather nervous.

There is a fifteen-minute break at ten o'clock during which only the loud-voiced flow of words of the *Staatsanwalt* is to be heard. His demand – four years in jail because of misusing the hospitality of the state, horror propaganda and instigation of the neighbors (the Netherlands) – is converted by the judges, after a six minute consideration, into an immaculately typed verdict: I am sentenced to eighteen months in jail with three months to count as served. No need to say that I felt both hot and cold in turn. The mere fact that the verdict is already typed up, proves clearly that this whole court procedure has been an act of camouflage. Everything had already been put on paper before the trial even started.

Before Raphael is brought back to his cell, he has to change his habit into brown prison clothes: he is considered a criminal prisoner now. After a couple of days, a police officer accompanies him to the railway station, where a train is going to bring him to Frankfurt.

For the first time in three months I see free people who can come and go as they please, kids laughing and playing, everything so common and yet so strange! At the railway station we have to wait for quite a while before the train with the prisoner-carriage arrives. I have never done the journey from Mainz to Frankfurt as cheap as this time, nor with such mixed feelings. I am not sitting on a padded bench now, but find myself instead in a compartment with hardly enough room for one person. It has a tiny windowpane with iron bars and thick, frosted glass. In Frankfurt, I am transferred to a prison van along with fifteen other prisoners. When we are all pushed inside, the doors close with a bang and, at full speed, we head in the direction of Preungesheim.

SURRENDER TO GOD'S WILL

There is a dim light shining down from the prison gate through which the car has entered. Another air-raid alarm sounds and everything is blacked out. On the way I overheard a conversation between the guards, stating how surprised they were "that those Tommys kept on coming, notwithstanding the strength of our *Luftwaffe*."

We are led across a large court, then up some broad stone stairs, whereupon doors are subsequently opened and locked behind us. In the end, we find ourselves in a wide hallway queuing up, waiting to be registered. Then each of us is put in a *Zugangszelle*. I am the last one.

The next morning all names are called over again and next we are taken into the *Hausväterei*, something like a tailor's shop. All of us receive blue-grey suits: coats without collar and trousers with a pocket hardly big enough for a handkerchief. Things are very worn out. On my "new" suit I can count up to 37 patches, from big to small, in many different colors.

After a couple of days, cell 58 is assigned to me. It looks like an exact copy of the one in Mainz that I described earlier, only this one is much neater.

As in Mainz, Raphael is put to work in the "paper bag manufacture" again, but this time the atmosphere is much more easy-going and he even gets paid—20 Pfennig per day! After three weeks he is summoned to the governor who informs him that as the only one of all foreign prisoners, he will be put to work outside his cell in a group of house painters. As a consequence he has to move to a smaller "Arbeiterzelle" since he is elsewhere during the day.

The cell that is allotted to me is only 15.8m³. With my fingertips I can touch both walls easily. The total width is no more than 1.70m. and the length six paces, the normal length of a cell. There is not much furniture either. It is small but clean and that is worth a lot. Instead of a wall-bed, it has a wooden berth that takes almost all the space. There is hardly any room left to go between bed and wall without touching the wall. At the head of the bed, underneath a small locker that hangs on the wall, is a small wooden table with a chair, at the foot of the bed the indispensable "little throne." A tiny narrow windowpane with thick bars lets in what air and light is needed. The floor is made of black painted cement and well scrubbed, so it looks spic-and-span all the time. The bowl, an aluminium basin, as well as the cutlery are always polished, shining like silver.

To me, this little cell becomes dear and beloved. Although there is not much room to live, I am very happy to be there. Sunday I have all to myself. I can do whatever I please—pray, read, pace up and down as much as I want. That is why this is the best day for me, even the Sundays when there is no Holy Mass. Then I stay still within myself, and the evening comes before I know!

My new job is with the house painters, a bunch of guys with conversations that make my hair stand up on end. It takes a lot of control not to run straightaway. However I have good hopes that I can do something good here, because the prison chaplain only comes to visit those who ask for him and my companions do not exactly belong to those people who have a desire for extra spiritual guidance. For the time being, I can get farthest by setting a good example and by a fervent and sincere prayer for these men who have sometimes fallen so low. Thank heaven, my prayers do not remain unheard.

For example, not one filthy word is spoken among my comrades after some time, and there is always a civil conversation going on during work.

Paul, one of the members of his work gang, is always seeking Raphael's company. When working together on the ladder or scaffold, he always steers the conversation in the direction of religion. He listens carefully to everything Raphael tells him and often asks for a joint prayer. Through the mediation of Raphael, the man gets permission to talk to the prison chaplain and to attend Mass too. On Christmas Day, when passing by Raphael, he whispers in his ear, "I have made my confession and next I will receive communion!"

To their great surprise, on Christmas Eve, all the prisoners receive a whole loaf of white bread and a sausage: for once this means going to bed without feeling hungry. The Christmas celebration has a special religious atmosphere as well. A huge lighted Christmas tree reaches high over the altar, Christmas carols are sung, and the words spoken by the prison chaplain touch many a heart of stone.

Every fortnight Holy Mass is celebrated, as I said before. We all sit in big wide benches set up like a stand. There is a simple altar with some flowers; a large stained glass window behind it represents the crucifixion. This is the only religious picture I have seen in all these days and I cannot stop myself from admiring a picture of such rare beauty. After the Gospel, the priest gives a short homily in which he tries to comfort us prisoners through warm words, heartening us with the help of the Gospel of that Sunday for the week to come, a week that will bring hours and days of darkness, which can be made fruitful in the spirit of the suffering Christ.

Back in my cell, I reflect on the words just heard and arrange my daily schedule according to them. The principle motivation that I keep my eyes set on is the thought of the suffering Christ. The scene in which the tyrants mock Jesus is my favorite subject matter during meditation. I also like to let the story from the Mount of Olives, where Jesus speaks the *fiat* to his Father in Heaven, pass through my mind. In my situation I still feel so small, and I try to say my *fiat* and accept everything that is happening to me as coming from the hand of the Lord. After that I can carry on despite all the crosses that are surely bound to come. Not a day passes without praying the Stations, and only by doing this over and over again one grows to love and value them more and more. That is how I spend most of my time as soon as I return from work, also sometimes by praying my Office. After supper I take a book and read for a while until the light is turned off. Then I do my evening prayers and lay myself to rest.

Of course we do the work we are supposed to do at the usual prison pace, that is to say, "what is not done today, will be finished tomorrow." It is one of the consequences of the reality that everything you do is only done to chase away boredom and kill time. Once we were to give the entire kitchen a new coat of paint, a job every prisoner would do "with enthusiasm," as far as one could speak of enthusiasm in our case. Hunger is the only motive that makes us so eager to work in the kitchen. The sergeant on duty, who is always present, is in many ways a reasonable man. He is "safe." Since during the day no other workmen are allowed in the kitchen except the cooks, the arrangement is that we will do our work in the night. During the night, besides checking on us a couple of times, the supervising night guards come for a cup of coffee or something else that we have made them. After they have left, making their rounds in the cold January night, we sit down at the table and put away a well-prepared meal by kind permission of the kitchen-sergeant, whose opinion it is that a workman should not be kept from his rightful deserts.

The kitchen is like an open house to the guards and we take advantage of this. For example, some 60 pigs died from swine-plague but passed by the inspector to be made into sausages. That is why during the day the cooks are working hard in their "sausage-factory." They use a cauldron that can manage 160 sausages at a time, but as a result of a small "error" in the addition, each time one or two additional sausages end up in the boiler. Those two are "accidentally" lost behind the boiler, where we happen to "find" them at night. In this way we manage to organize, as we call it, seven sausages. The next thing is to get these seven "boys" into our workshop. For that, we decide to use our friend Topf – that is the guard's name – on one of his patrol rounds. At one o'clock in the night when he comes to the kitchen for his usual cup of coffee, one of us asks him if he would be so kind to open the doors and gates that separate us from the workshop, since we have to take a tool box in there. Without hesitation, Topf is willing to come along and open the doors. Seeing how heavy the "tools" are weighing on our companion, he says, "Come, let us carry that together. That is much better." Together with the sergeant we see him and the seven sausages disappear in the dark of the night, on their way to the workshop, where some of our hungry comrades receive an extra ration the next day! This happened for one month and during that time none of us lost one ounce in weight!

As a consequence of this kitchen job, our cells are searched every day for possible illegal foods that might be present. The guard has a little way of throwing the entire contents about the cell, as if there had been an earthquake. It is almost impossible to open the cell door. Of course everything has to be tidy within the twinkling of an eye, even if the bed has been pulled apart, the straw mattress taken out and put against the back wall, chair put on top of the locker, table on top of the bed, etc. I am always careful that nothing illicit will be found in my cell. Whatever we take from the kitchen illegally is distributed in the workshop among the rest of us straight away.

Another constant serious danger is smoking, strictly forbidden but for many of us a daily "crime." I would have loved to smoke a cigarette with the others, but I resign myself not to out of precaution, although none of my companions could understand why I never smoked, being a Dutchman. I did however manage to give them a light – need is the mother of invention – in the following way. First of all, we got our hands on a small flint that we hid in a pencil. With an old razor blade we scratched some celluloid off an old toothbrush and then we stroked a spark out of the flint, also with the razor blade. As soon as a spark hit the celluloid, it caught fire that, in turn, set fire to a small piece of paper. This then was used to light the cigarette, meant for those of us dying for a smoke.

Breaking the non-smoking rule leads to an automatic three days in the "bunker." This penalty meant intensified solitary confinement, water and bread and no straw mattress. I use great care not to break the governor's favorite rule, so I decide to quit smoking during the time of my stay. The governor once told me that if ever I did something wrong, I would not only be punished, but the punishment would be seven times worse than that given any other person. So that makes me very careful indeed!

Most of the guards are well disposed to the prisoners, especially those who are the craftsmen, except for one guard, who is to be avoided as much as possible. One day this "hunter" stopped me, saying, "You are a Dutchman, are you not?" After I answer in the affirmative, he takes me to a distant corner where there is no breeze, even though we happen to be outside. Then he takes my hand and starts sniffing my fingers carefully, looking at me with sharp eyes, and he says, "*Da haben Sie Schwein gehabt!*" Yes indeed, I was definitely lucky that time. He suspected me, being Dutch, to be a smoker and he would have loved to report me to the governor, but he had to let me go without catching me breaking the rules. At night, when the lights are low and each of us is in bed, he walks past the cells with felt slippers on, sniffing at keyholes to catch the smell of someone smoking! This creature is a horrible person even in the eyes of his colleagues. No other guard is such a stickler for regulations and discipline the way he is as none of them sympathizes with the Nazis.

Not only because of smoking offences does one run the risk of ending up in the bunker, but also by having political conversations or putting statements of any kind in the biography that one has to write at arrival. Raphael mentions the one time when he had to number the toilets in all the cells with black paint. In one of the cells a newcomer is working on his résumé and to make sure he did right, he starts reading it out to Raphael. He appears to be a member of a group most hated by the Nazis, the Bibelforchers or Jehovah's Witnesses. They have the peculiar habit of explaining the Bible, especially the Old Testament, from a political point of view. In this way they pretend to know exactly how long Hitler will stay in power, et cetera. No wonder the Nazis dislike them so much and in prisons and camps they have a very hard time, no less difficult than the Jews and the clergy.

"In my opinion," the man writes, "Adolf Hitler is a person sent by God, but, I think he is like a new broom. A new broom is honored as long as it is new. Once it has been used for some time, it is considered useless and put in a corner. The same thing will happen to Hitler. First people will think all the world of him, until one day they will not take any notice of him!" As I hear him read aloud these words, I advise him strongly to give up his intention to hand over this piece of paper, because the governor will not hesitate one second to send him straightaway to the bunker. However, he sticks to his conviction of which he is not at all ashamed. No need to say that he gets to know the bunker soon. One day I can hear the governor yelling and screaming at him in his cell when he is visiting him along with a high ranking official. "If I had an ax right now, I would cleave your skull personally."

Also the Poles are having a hard time. On the day they arrive, they get a 21-day confinement and, after that, they have to do the heaviest work of all, the so-called *Stanzen*. This is extremely heavy, because one has to chop at least two thousand, sometimes six thousand pieces of leather with a heavy hammer and chisel specially designed for the job. In the dark cells in the basement the only thing heard is the continuous hammering of the *Stanzers*. Everyone with an arrest ends up with the *Stanzers* afterwards, all the more proof that this is considered heavy work by the authorities as well.

After a while, Raphael is assigned to the fire brigade and transferred to a cell one floor below. Every Saturday afternoon a fire-drill is held, sometimes near the houses of the officials, other times in the women's section of the prison. As soon as the prisoners arrive, Raphael hears the female guard shout to their amusement, "Alles einrücken, Männer kommen!" All the women that happen to be present in the hallway have to stand facing the wall until the fire brigade has passed. To Raphael, it is as if he is in a nunnery!

Behind the women's section of the prison is the highest radio tower of Frankfurt's broadcasting station. During one of the many night air raids on Mainz and Frankfurt, the British have dropped a bomb just behind the tower causing considerable damage to any glass in the prison and a lot of material devastation to the houses. However, it causes no personal injury among the prisoners. While the firemen are waiting for the order '*Ausrücken*', the commander makes the superfluous remark that anyone who uses the darkness of the night as a means to escape, will be shot on sight. Often I have had opportunity to escape. But it never seriously occurred to me, since the consequences would be out of proportion, as experience taught us.

I decide to accept my fate. Surrendering to God's Holy Will is much better than escaping. Turning the loss of freedom, the greatest good mankind has, into an offering must be pleasing to the good Lord, I am sure. So I make it a habit, almost second nature, to do a short act of surrender to the good Lord in my mind, or simply, a quick prayer like "Everything for You, my Jesus" each time the clock in the prison tower announces a new quarter hour. This I can do without anyone noticing.

In the end, Raphael remains imprisoned in Pre-ungesheim for fourteen months. Although he makes mention of air raids only a couple of times, there is no doubt that they must have meant very terrifying hours for him and the other prisoners. The doors were unbolted at the hall side to allow for immediate action in case of an emergency, but they remain locked. In the monotonous world of prison life, everything that happens outside the prison becomes unreal. It is as if war and its predicaments hardly affect Raphael. He is a prisoner cut off from the outside world.

Impressions of the prison have a much greater impact on him. For the first time in his life he is confronted with death in an extremely cruel manner. Preungesheim happens to be one of the prisons where death penalties are carried out by means of the guillotine. During the years of the Fascists' regime, hundreds of German and foreign resistance fighters are executed. The bodies of these victims of Nazi terror disappear into university medical clinics for anatomical research. The Deliquentzelle, *where the condemned persons wait for the sentence to be carried out, is never empty. During Raphael's imprisonment, some 28 men and women are put to death. Raphael is deeply affected. He describes extensively and in minute detail the way an execution takes place and how the condemned person passes the last night. He tells about a man who, once his time had come, said to the prison chaplain, "Do not bother, Father. In five minutes I will be talking with the good Lord himself."*

The other prisoners live with the thought that they will be free soon. In the morning, prisoners greet each other saying "Good morning! Another 96 days." "Good morning," is the reply, "another 37 days!"

When Raphael's sentence is nearly completed, the Gestapo in the Netherlands arrests one of his fellow Carmelites in the Carmelite monastery of Nijmegen on suspicion of Deutschfeindliche activities. It is Father Titus Brandsma, the 61 year old professor of philosophy and former rector of the Catholic University of Nijmegen (now Radboud University). During Brandsma's busy and active life, he is among those responsible for the reopening of the Carmelite monastery in Mainz, the place where Raphael was arrested eighteen months before.

Titus Brandsma's fight for the right to educate Jewish children and freedom of the press has been a thorn in the flesh of the Germans for quite some time. His unshakeable "no" to the occupying force, when they demand that Catholic newspapers should accept Nazi propaganda, infuriates the Nazis. On January 19, 1942, he is arrested. That day marks the beginning of a long agony that starts in the prison of Scheveningen, continues in the transit camp of Amersfoort and the prison of Kleve, and ends in the concentration camp in Dachau.

Finally, January 31, 1942, the court date, has arrived. It is the day when I hope to return to the monastery in Mainz. The day takes a different course, however, much different from what I expected.

In the morning, while the rest of my comrades are gathered at the *Centrale* to march out to work, I am waiting, with a bundle under my arm, with a few other lucky ones who will also be released, waving another sincere farewell to those who are staying behind. As they go out to work, we are taken downstairs to the storeroom where our clothes were kept but are now returned to us. After each of us has exchanged his prison clothes for his civilian ones, and we all look like decent civilians again, we are called into the office to sign some paperwork. Tension is rising by the minute. Freedom is coming closer and closer. Another couple of moments… When it is my turn and I am completely dressed in my own things, a guard takes me into the so-called *Abgangszelle* where prisoners have to wait until the final signal of departure is given.

Meanwhile it is almost nine o'clock when the door opens and I can go upstairs. I think the moment of my release has come, and I follow the guard cheerfully to the "second gate." Here I am left in a small parlor, the guard leaves, and the door is locked. That must be the force of habit, I think to myself, whenever such a man goes out of doors, he is inclined to lock them without thinking. As far as I am concerned, I see myself locked up in this room as a free man, but nobody comes. Finally I grow a little impatient and start knocking when I hear someone passing by. The guard who opens the door tells me a car will arrive any minute to take me away, and I am so naïve as to believe that a private car will come and take me to Mainz.

It is getting late. Another hour has gone by and still no car has arrived, and again I start knocking on the door when I hear footsteps in the hallway. The door opens and the laughing face of the prison chaplain appears. "Dear me, are you still here?" he asks. "Yes, Father, how come I am still not a free man?" The priest stays for a chat and wishes me a safe journey home. According to him there are no more difficulties to fear. He has just seen my certificate, signed by the governor, and it is drawn up in such a way that I have nothing to fear from any Gestapo. Before dawn I will have returned to the monastery! These and other words give me courage again and I wait patiently. It is afternoon now, but still no car. Suddenly the door opens again and I expect to hear my name. But no, in the doorway stands a guard with a prisoner carrying a bowl with some food. This will be my last meal in prison, my farewell dinner.

By the end of the afternoon, mention is made of the arrival of a car. A senior guard opens the little room and after he has handed over a receipt for the wages for my work—about 104 Marks—at the counter, he walks me over the large inner court to the "first gate," where he cancels me as a "resident." As I am standing outside the gate, the long expected vehicle arrives. My heart almost sinks into my boots when I see the green police van. There she is again—the usual paddy wagon! They push me into the one remaining seat left; the other passengers are women from various detention centers and prisons.

After a half-hour drive we arrive in the center of Frankfurt. We stop at Starkegasse, at the police station, and get out of the car. Being the only male prisoner, I have to wait at the side before they call me in. After having given my name, date of birth, place of birth, *et cetera*, for the hundredth time, I am taken to a cell, alone. The only furniture I see is a long bench, and I sit down for a while, debating inwardly what should happen next. Then the thought shoots through my mind that I will probably have to hand over all my stuff again, and this time I want to try and keep my rosary and the small prayer-book that I got back that morning. So I hasten to take both of them out of my briefcase. I am able to do that just in time. The cell door opens and I have to follow. Back in the office where I had been just before, I have to put all my belongings on the table and an accurate list is made that I have to sign. Even my suspenders have to be handed over to prevent a possible suicide attempt. Everything goes into a small bag and I stand with my hands on my trousers to stop them from falling down!

Next, a guard accompanies me to a large cell, so pitch dark that, at first, I cannot see where I am. There are eleven iron cages, and I am put in one of them. A narrow iron gate is the entrance to this place of "residence" of about 2.5 meters in length and 1.75 meters wide; the sidewalls are made of solid plating, the front, as well as the top, are made of heavy iron wire netting. When the guard has locked me up and leaves, I hear voices coming from all sides. I am not the only one in this dark and obscure place. I get used to the darkness after a while and I am able to distinguish a vague silhouette of someone opposite my cage—a Swiss man. Further away, in the same sort of "lion" cages are two Italians, someone from Belgium, two Frenchmen and four Germans, among them three Jews. All together there are eleven of us, a motley group. As I have considered myself a free man since this morning, I do not feel at ease here at all. However, there is not much I can do about it and I am resigned to the inevitable again. In the monastery in Mainz, they were expecting me this very day. Now everything has changed, more changed than anyone could have imagined.

All day long the bench, that is to serve more or less as a couch, is fixed to the wall by a chain, making it impossible to stretch out and rest. Only the small shelf that serves as a table provides any opportunity to sit.

Days last forever here since there is no distraction at all apart from the constant murmuring of those who communicate their adventures. What remains is the nerve-racking waiting in this dark cage.

The food that is handed out is not exactly excessive. Two different portions are offered, the so-called large and small portion. The small one is meant for the one who has just arrived. The large one goes to those who are being detained for over seven days, although the Jews only get a small portion, irrespective of the length of their stay. The difference is no more than a spoonful of marmalade to go with the bread and the lump of bread, or better the slice, is a little bit thicker. Early in the morning, a row of mugs filled with black coffee is waiting for us. As soon as we are ordered outside, each of us may pick a mug from the stone floor after having said his name and receive his portion of bread with or without the bonus portion. The afternoon brings some jacket boiled potatoes and a spoonful of vegetables, sometimes a bit of cabbage soup. In the evening there is half a liter of floury soup. It is not much at all and a feeling of constant hunger is something we all share.

I understand from my fellow-prisoners that the length of time one has to stay in these cages varies. There are the lucky ones who leave within three days, while others leave after a week. Yet some of us have been here for seventeen days already and see no end to it. As a rule, however, most residents are gone within three to seven days. Thus my hope is that the third day will be my last day. Indeed, by the evening, the door swings open and an official calls my name. Since it is pitch-dark in the cell, he cannot see me, so I keep calling "here" until he stands in front of my cage. Then he opens a large book with a form I have to sign. Apparently it has something to do with the amount of money that I had handed over three days ago. It will be sent to me by mail now. Because it is impossible to see anything, he strikes a match and I can read that the name Darmstadt is written behind my name and the amount of money to be transferred. I tell the official that the money has to be sent to Mainz instead of Darmstadt, since I live in the aforementioned town. The official is convinced that it is all right as it is, or else he will look over it later; after saying this he leaves. Since I had signed everything, I was sure things were beginning to move, and whether the money would be sent to Mainz or Darmstadt was the same to me as long as I was going to reach Mainz!

They wake us very early the next morning. Some of us, including me, are chased out of our cages. In the beginning, we stand in the hallway for quite a while, but finally we are let into the office one by one. We receive our things and sign for them. I also have my suspenders back again. I use the opportunity to ask one of the officials what my situation is and if I am to be allowed to go home now. After all, in my opinion, I have already been a free man for three days! The sergeant starts shouting at me, demanding how on earth I have the nerve to ask such a question. I will get a "free ticket" for sure! I return to my place among the others in the hallway, waiting for something to happen.

After everything is done, we are pushed into the Black Maria again. This time we are heading for the train station. When we get there, a group of *Schupos* (*Schutzpolizei* or Municipal Police) is waiting for us, and they take us to a large locked room, with no light and little ventilation. The dark of the night surrounds us when the heavy steel door closes with a bang. The best thing to do is just to stand still since it is impossible to see where one is. All of a sudden someone grasps my arm and asks me who I am. It is an elderly man from Preungesheim like me. That is why he stays with me, he is almost overcome by his nerves.

The Nazis are masters in increasing uncertainty in those who are in their power. The continual signing up and signing out, handing over things and receiving them back again, loads of official documents that have to be signed without knowing what they are about, no information about what will happen and endless waiting in bad conditions wear a man down and put his nerves to the test. Raphael's adventures are a powerful example of this and still there is no end in sight. The strength with which Raphael persists in the idea that he is a free man is striking, although all the signals indicate that the worst is yet to come.

After a while the door opens and we are ordered outside. Again we are on the platform where a row of policemen with guns on their shoulders are standing, accompanied by a bunch of watchdogs. We walk between the rows, and observed with curious looks by hundreds of people waiting on the platform for their trains, we arrive at the train that is going to take us to… we do not know where yet! While I am led through that busy terminal, together with all sorts of low lifes between two rows of armed police, a strange feeling comes over me in spite of myself. Although the next time, I can cope with it better. You get used to everything.

The special carriage for prisoners, always attached to any train, is already waiting for its new passengers. We get on and are divided into several groups, depending

on how many a compartment can take. The old fellow
is still standing next to me, and we end up together in
a little cell where a few others have already been
placed. One is from this prison, the other from that
detention house, a third one has to do some time in
one or the other "boarding houses," and so on. Nobody knows in which direction we are going, because
our carriage is hooked on after we boarded.

Anyway, the train starts to roll and we are on our
way. "Lets hope for the best," we tell each other, "and it
is a free ride after all!" The cosiness in the cabin keeps
us from worrying too much, and after many stops we
end up in another huge station, the station of Darmstadt, where we get off the train.

ENCOUNTERING
THE HORRIBLE MONSTER "DEATH"

The police officer who "receives" us in Darmstadt starts making clear to us how senseless it is to escape, since we knew very well what the consequences would be. In other words, we would be shot immediately. Then we are taken to the police office at the station, where we are lined up in groups. One of the officers carries a handful of consignment-notes, plain consignment-notes. We are sent off in exactly the same way and with the same forms as goods! In our group is a young girl, nearly twenty years old. As they read her consignment note, she is put aside like me. The men are scrutinizing us one by one. One boy draws their attention. I am able to catch some comments about him, which are not good for him. Mention is made of concentration camps.

The man with the forms, opposite me, looks somewhat pleasant. So I pull myself together again. Despite that earlier in the morning I was told explicitly never to address these "great lords," I ask him what my situation is and if I am to go home soon. He looks up from the consignment-note and, to my great joy, he tells me that I have only been taken here to go through certain formalities. "This very evening you shall be home," he says.

Finally we get into the police car that stands ready and, in an open van, we drive through the streets of the busy town. It has been a long time since I saw people walking in the streets without being harassed—free people in other words. How different they are from us

who are still in chains. The car stops at several police
stations but each time the answer is: "*Der Holländer
gehört nicht hierhin, dessen Name ist bei uns nicht einge-
tragen!*" (The Dutchman does not belong here; his
name is not registered in our office). I keep on hoping
from the depths of my heart that I will not "belong"
anywhere in the end and that I will arrive safe and
sound in the monastery in Mainz in the evening. But
again I am bitterly disappointed. After a lot of cross
talk, they manage to find a door that opens for me! I
end up in the Round Tower, a big old building. Upstairs a prisoner is scrubbing and I ask him what is going on here. "Oh," he says, "it is okay. You will be fine
here." I tell him I am no wiser for his answer. Timidly,
he looks around him, whispering, "Gestapo." I know
enough now.

After I have waited in the hallway for a while, they
let me in. Mister Gestapo is sitting behind his desk in
his plain clothes. In a corner behind a small table is a
prisoner who apparently belongs on the staff. Again I
go through the perpetual giving of name, etc. When I
am done, I have to hand over all my stuff to the prisoner. Everything is registered and put in a bag with the
exception of … my shaving-brush. I draw his attention
to this in case he might have forgotten it. No, the shaving-brush is for me to keep. "Then you might as well
give me back my razor. Just the brush is no good to
me," I say. But that is not allowed. Shaving will be tak-
en care of. I manage to hold back the rosary and
church booklet that I rescued just in time from my
briefcase in Frankfurt. These turned out to be very use-
ful in my cell. They would be my one and only consolation in the weeks to come.

Once again Raphael is put under lock and key: for more than four weeks, he and three other prisoners share a small cell at the Gestapo office in Darmstadt. During that time, they are allowed out only three times for one quarter of an hour. Tension for these prisoners is so much higher than for those who stay in a normal prison, because the latter know when their confinement will be over. Here nobody knows what is going on and why they are still detained.

A fortnight goes by before I am granted permission to give notice to the monastery in Mainz that I am being held at the Gestapo office in Darmstadt. Finally they learn were I have been since my "release"! Except for my ups and downs, I let them know that we are allowed a visit every now and then and food parcels up to one kilo.

Soon a visitor arrives in the person of Mrs Kronebach, the organist's wife. Since the outbreak of the war, my brothers in Mainz, being Dutch, are no longer allowed to leave the town. She arrives on a Tuesday afternoon. Since Tuesday is not a visiting day, they do not let her in. It takes her a lot of effort to get permission to leave her sandwiches behind. When they are brought to our cell, where the four of us—equally starving—pass the day by telling each other stories, they are gobbled up in a minute.

With great trouble Mrs Kronebach succeeds in getting a permit to visit me the next afternoon. The day before, I had prepared myself very well for the visit in order to discuss everything that is necessary. I had drawn up a detailed letter, written in very small print on three cigarette papers and folded many times. It had all kinds of instructions to the prior. For instance,

I told him how to read a letter of mine in case I ended up somewhere where it would not be possible to write honestly and truthfully, like a concentration camp or someplace similar.

The following afternoon, Mrs. Kronebach is waiting in the office of the Gestapo when they call me. The moment I enter, she makes a few steps in my direction and starts to cry immediately. She takes her handkerchief out of her handbag, and while I keep the little note in my hand as a tiny ball of paper, I try to calm her down and walk towards her. When she holds out her hand to me, I had already slipped the note into her handbag without the Gestapo man noticing. A while later I receive a reply to my clandestine note. Certainly it is a comfort to me to know that they understood. It was a small preparation anyway.

After some days, I again have a visitor. This time it is a lawyer. I tell him straight out that I fear I will end up in a concentration camp. One of my cellmates has spent nine months in Dachau already. So I have an idea, more or less, of what it is like there.

The lawyer can do no more for Raphael than to leave his packet of sandwiches behind. Then, some weeks later, Raphael is called to the office of the Gestapo again to sign his Schutzhaftbefehl *(warrant). At a glance, Raphael reads the reason for his continuing imprisonment: "Danger of possible political actions when released early. Signed: Heydrich, head of Gestapo."*

I realise my fate is sealed with or without my name on this blood red piece of paper, and that is why I scratch my name, with a bad pen, in the assigned space. Certainly I have many feelings. It is very clear to me that this is, beyond any doubt, the beginning of a long, and thank God, at the time still unknown how long, road to Calvary. I ask the Gestapo man what "early release" means. "Till the end of the war and then maybe some more weeks…" It was little comfort but things came true exactly as he said, only in a slightly different manner than he thought.

I am sent back to my cell, but after half an hour the door opens and the person entering comes with the message that, if I prefer not to, I do not have to go to Dachau! "How come?" I ask, "Is there still a chance to get out of all this?" Now that I have signed my name to the *Schutzhaftbefehl*, the case seems to be settled for me. "Oh," he replies, "you are wearing a habit, are you not. When you decide to hang it on a hat-rack, nothing will happen to you. You can get a hell-of-a-job right here and everything will be fine!" "Well, tell your boss that under such conditions, I would rather go to Dachau and that I stand by my signature!" The other cell inmates, although none of them is a Catholic, think it is an extraordinary piece of Gestapo technique to attack a person at his deepest convictions in a moment when he is about to encounter the horrible monster "death" that lies in wait in the concentration camp. I take my rosary and pray to Heaven for the mercy of assistance and strength in all the difficulties and dangers yet to be sustained and conquered.

During our stay in the Round Tower in Darmstadt there are no distractions such as books or work of any kind. We chat all the time and, sometimes, we enjoy ourselves with playing some game, made of a piece of cardboard. Of course, this is strictly forbidden, but the Gestapo has never discovered anything. One of us keeps a good watch, with his ear against the door, to listen for anyone approaching. One day after another passes without any change in our situation. Not every change is an improvement. That is for sure. Nevertheless, we wait each day for something to happen. Finally a cold Thursday, March 12, 1942, brings that change.

The door swings open and the floor-guard, a prisoner like me, is standing in the doorway with potatoes boiled in their jackets and a bowl of red beets in his hands. It is our last dinner and we have to hurry as the transport is about to leave any minute. Quickly, we make short work of the sober meal and wait for the order to go downstairs. When everything is ready for our departure, there are eight of us that will be put on transport. Each person receives one loaf of bread to eat on the way, which makes us think that the journey ahead of us will be a long one.

Next we get in the police car that stands ready to take us to the train station, where the train with the special prisoners' car is waiting for us already. After all of us are "loaded," the train begins to move and pulls out in the direction of Dachau. Although the train stops a couple of times, the distance of only 60 miles is soon covered. By seven o'clock we arrive in Würzburg. The train has not even stopped yet, when they already put us in irons two and two. This is the first and last time that I have felt shackles around my wrists. In rows of two, we have to get off the train to go in front of the station, where a small van for eight persons is waiting. My companion on my right hand side is very depressed by the fact that he is led in public like a dangerous criminal through such a crowded station. All my attempts to comfort him are in vain. He keeps feeling despised and expelled. At this moment, my thoughts go to the greatest chained Sufferer, Jesus

Christ: was He not a thousand times more innocent than me! Did He not let Himself be put into chains under totally different circumstances?! This thought consoles me exceedingly and so for Him I love to be bound with a couple of visible fetters. I am pulled from my reflections by a guard giving me a push as an invitation to get in the car. It is a small, green police van with eight seats, only now twenty of us are squeezed into it. Chained to each other, we lean and squat over each other. It is a good thing the trip does not take long. We are not even leaving town.

In the prison of Würzburg, the entire group is put in one cell and after some soup and bread, and after a lot of pinching and scraping, they lay themselves to rest on the five (!) straw-mattresses that are present in the cell.

Thursday, March 12 also brings a big change for Titus Brandsma, who had been imprisoned in Scheveningen since January 19, 1942. In the early morning of that day – he is busy writing the biography of Teresa of Avila, someone enters his cell. "On behalf of the General-Chief of the Security Police and Security Services I must invite you, Professor Doctor Brandsma, to come along with me at once. We are going to Amersfoort. The car is already waiting."

The period in which Brandsma is alone in his cell, when he writes a beautiful poem, a clear and sharp apologia*, as well as seven chapters on the life of St. Teresa, comes to an abrupt ending. In the notorious transit camp of Amersfoort, where the most feared camp-commander Berg wields the sceptre, the fragile health of the 61-year old Carmelite priest diminishes rapidly. Extremely hard circumstances, heavy labor, malnutrition, and dysentery make a physical wreck out of him, but fail to break his strength of mind.*

Early next morning they wake us up. All of us are put in irons again, but as I stretch out my wrists to be chained to my friend like yesterday, the official on duty says, "This gentleman can step back to the end of the row. He will find a colleague of his over there. The clergy must travel unchained." I walk towards the end of the row and see a man that appears, by his dress, to be a pastor. I say hello and he introduces himself as *Pfarrer* (Pastor) Hermann Quack from Maximilianau in the neighborhood of Trier. From that moment, we stay together and wait until everyone else is chained. Next we are taken to the train station in the vans that are already waiting for us. Both of us can sit in the front next to a driver, and thanks to the kindness of these police officers, we do not have to sit with the rest in the back of the prisoners' van. On the way, I hear that there are two more clergymen among us, so that makes four of us.

At the station we meet Dr. Hans Carls, the *Caritas* director from Wuppertal and the Pallottine priest, Joseph Kentenich, from Schönstatt. The latter is rather famous, not only in clergy circles where he has given many retreats, but above all and especially because he is the pioneer of the radio broadcast *Schönstadt-Bewegung*—the special devotion to Mary, Mother of God under the title *Ter Admirabilis* (Thrice Admirable). The four of us are crammed into a small cabin of 75 cm^3, with only one small bench and a little shelve that serves as a table in a normal compartment. The *Caritas* director and the Pallottine priest, both elderly gentlemen, sit next to each other on the bench, while Pastor Quack sits down on the table. From Würzburg to Dachau is about 300 miles. Notwithstanding the cold of March, it is very hot and oppressive in this small cabin, which makes us all terribly thirsty. Luckily, there is a bucket full of water going round and everyone can quench his thirst.

Despite the lack of space, the mood is still cheerful. The priest turns out to be a pretty good poet and keeps reciting poems on Mary, which whiles away time and brightens up the monotony of such a transport. The director, a rather corpulent man and a nice man as well, is cracking the funniest jokes in between the poetry of Father Kentenich and gives us a good laugh. Underneath the wide rim of his hat not only long silver-white hairs appear but also big sweat-drops, as if he is on fire. Pastor Quack, a quiet, kind-hearted man, as I came to experience several times in Dachau, decides to close his breviary since there is too much laughing. Suddenly, our enjoyable storyteller bursts out in tears, thinking of the past weeks when he was locked up in prison in Wuppertal, in an anxious and nerve-wrecking wait for what would happen next, and how from time to time his secretary managed to smuggle in Our Lord in a matchbox.

By five o'clock we are approaching the station of Dachau. The concentration camp, at least the location of the barracks, becomes visible from a mile outside of the town. Some of us stand on our toes to reach the small barred windows, but I cannot be bothered. I will have to be there long enough, I am thinking. I stand still until the train stops and we are ordered to get out. Finally, we have arrived in the infamous town of Dachau!

IT IS NOT A LONG WAY
TO THE CREMATORIUM

There is a large truck full of SS officers on the platform, harsh voices are sounding, and our exiting the train is not going quickly enough apparently, although it happens head over heels. The moment I step from the footboard onto the platform, I get a kick from an iron-tipped shoe in such a way that I hurtle into the car with a bound. Well, that is a great start, I think, and look for a seat in the truck where I am not too close to such a person. Off we go, leaving the platform at full speed while terrified looking people watch us.

The camp is situated some miles away from the station and on the way we notice the first *Häftlingen* in their striped prison uniforms, best described as "zebra." From now on we are only called *Häftlingen*. Prisoner is not what we are. Life in the camp is not a prisoner's life. According to the SS, it is all a matter of *Umschulung* (re-education)!

After some minutes, we arrive at the camp itself. The heavy iron gates swing open and more screaming voices: *aussteigen*! It is March 13 and bitterly cold as a rough wind skims the barracks and snow is cracking under our feet. Estranged, shy, and even a bit anxious, we have a quick look around, but there is not much time allowed. On we go again, this time to the *Schubraum*, which means something like a reception office. In the *Schubraum*, other prisoners who are put to work there are waiting for us. The only thing the SS man does is walk around a bit, uttering a curse or some sarcastic remark, especially to the clergy who, like the rest, are ordered to undress and stand next to their heap of clothes until it is their turn. Of course, everybody must give his complete family-register to begin with and sign for whatever valuables he is carrying. The items are put in a big, numbered paper bag, together with shoes and clothing. We are told to remember that number, and all of us receive a note with the number on it. My number is 29388. Twenty-nine three eighty-eight. It might as well be a phone-number!

Next, we head towards the bathhouse, a large hall with showers attached onto the many pipes that run through the place at a height of several meters. There some barbers wait for us to "help" us get rid of each single hair on our body in a rude and careless way. Each person gets a small piece of soap, but first he has to pass by someone holding a bucket of water mixed with a large quantity of Lysol. This is smeared all over our bodies with a big brush, an awfully painful experience. The Lysol and water makes the freshly depilated body sting to such a degree that you do not know where to turn. All this is happening under scornful laughter of SS men who stand and watch. Not satisfied with the treatment yet and before we are allowed to take a shower, we have to plunge into a large tub filled with the same biting, stinging fluid. Apparently I have not immersed all over, for when I come to the surface an SS man beats me on the head so that I almost faint and disappear in the tub once again. Writhing with pain, I crawl out after a careful look to make sure the SS man has gone.

We finally have our shower, and things get better as soon as the stinging Lysol is gone. Everyone gets a towel and a set of worn-out clothes. Thank God we have something to shield us from the looks of the SS. Father Kentenich approaches me, but I do not recognize him: shaven all over, hair cropped-close like me, he stands before me, his beautiful silver-grey beard a victim of the scissors as well. In less than half an hour, we have all become unrecognisable, wrapped in rags, worse than a beggar in the street. On my new jacket one can count "only" 37 patches, just like the uniform I once had in Preungesheim.

After all of us are clothed "in new," they take us to the *Zugangsblock* (admission block). By the time we get there, it is long into the evening and not much time is left. Within minutes though, they have assigned each person to a bunk bed. The size of the dormitory is about 9 to10 meters and there are 100 bunk beds altogether, standing three high. Each bed has a straw-mattress, two blankets, and a sheet. (Later on, there were no more sheets. They were probably used to help the war victims.) The living quarters are roughly the same size and have 9 or 10 large tables. So-called *Spinden*, small lockers—about 55 in total—hang all around on the walls. In the middle of the *Stube* (living room) stands a huge masonry tile-kiln German style. Because of all this furniture, there is not much room left, and yet in normal circumstances 100 people are living here. Much later, when the population of the camp increased daily, it accomodated 370, and in some even 500 or more were put up. It is not hard to imagine the way we "lived" here!

During the first days everything in these new surroundings is rather strange. Whatever you do here has to be done at full speed, which goes for everything in the camp. All day long we are busy learning camp songs, the meaning of military SS insignia, making beds in a senseless way, cleaning lockers and floors, *et cetera*. Learning how to march correctly, sometimes for over eight hours in a single day, is also part of our daily program.

All the barracks have a *Blockälteste* (head of the barracks). In each of the four quarters (*Stuben*), a *Stubenälteste* is in charge. Until the end of 1944, most of the time, low grade professional criminals held these jobs. In the admission block, *Käse-Hannes* from Nürnberg is our room elder. He has that nickname because he used to be a local dealer in cheese. This man has been convicted for criminal offences some 23 times. That says it all. This "king" reigns over some hundreds of priests: chaplains, pastors, deans, even an orthodox bishop are his subjects. He is not so bad after all, I must admit, as long as he is treated to all kinds of dainties and bacon that came later on in our food parcels.

For the first time, we have to attend main roll call. Among the newcomers are four priests and, although no one knows us, from a great distance we see a priest stretch out his hands in blessing. Hour after hour, we stand outside in the rain and bitter cold in rows of ten, not knowing what the waiting is about. The *Caritas* director asks for the umpteenth time: "But what are we waiting for anyway?" None of us knows the answer. Finally, the *Arbeitseinsatzdienstführer* (chief of work) arrives, a young SS fellow with a flat cap and a couple of stars on his collar. In the beginning, we dreaded such "high gents" more or less. He walks in between the rows, asking everybody what his profession is in civil life. As soon as he finds out that one or the other is a priest or religious, a series of provocations and mockery follow. "Are you married? How many women did you keep? You did have a housekeeper, did you not? How many bastard children do you have anyway?" Then all newcomers have to step forward at the main entrance of the camp, where *Herr Lagerkommandant* (camp commander) is going to speak. Again we wait several hours until the SS man deigns to appear on the scene. We are lined up according to nationality with exception of the clergy. They form a separate group. With a raw, drunk voice, he stands before us, putting forward a theory that makes many a man's hair stand on end. The speech has to be translated by the *Dolmetscher* (interpreter) in various languages straight away. Using coarse, rude, vulgar words, he calls us the dregs of society, we are expelled from the nation, not worth living, just good enough to be hanged; and for the rest, we should never forget that it is not a long way to the crematorium. "You can see the chimney over there," and he points with his finger in its direction at the same time.

After the "ceremony," *Herr Kommandant* walks past the rows and stops at our group, of course, to hurl all kinds of abuse in our faces. A prisoner is standing next to the *Lagerführer*, a band around his arm with the word *Lagerälteste* (camp elder). It is his duty to carry out all orders of the SS in an accurate way, which he does so meticulously it makes us quiver. Everybody knows who he is, the notorious "Kap Martin" and later there was "Kap Wagner." Their roaring voices ring out during roll call. They are communists, prisoners like we are, but they make us suffer the most. They are willing tools in the hands of the SS, even surpassing them in their beastly behavior. This is all the more horrible when you come to realize that we have to live with them on a day-to-day basis. The SS beat us as it is. The communists, though, beat us much more and worse. They hit us and kick us till we drop and find devilish pleasure in kicking our stomachs until they get tired. How we got to know the communists! They even steal the little, inadequate food of their fellow prisoners who are left to their mercy and will. Their device is "Your death is our life."

Inside the barracks, the *Stubenältesten* rule. In their hands, the continuously used club was a sign of their dignity. How many priests have I seen beaten up, worse than a dog? In the beginning, when I was not quite familiar with their brutal methods yet, I used to hide in a corner or behind a door as soon as I saw a priest being whacked, and cry bitterly at the thought of Christ being so dishonored in his priests. Once, I happened to be hiding in the washing room when a young Polish priest saw me and asked what was wrong. I told him what I had seen, and as an answer he let me know that this is a daily routine and that I would soon find out for myself. Soon it was that I found out. I get beaten up every day, not just once but sometimes even more!

The degree to which the priests suffer is enormous. Holy Week is an opportunity to treat the priests even more cruelly and degradingly. It is a real Passion Week and many do not survive the torments. For eight days, from Palm Sunday till Easter Monday, there are punishment-drills in the roll call square and in the streets of the camp.

It is the Monday of Holy Week, March 30. After two weeks in the Admission Block, I am transferred to Block 28. This barracks, where mainly Polish priests are living, is being collectively punished just as I arrive because somebody had not obeyed the order to hand over all their money. Whoever witnessed this will never be able to forget. It is as if the devil himself is making the rounds! To begin with, hundreds of priests, regardless of age or health conditions, have to stand for several hours, completely undressed, outside in the streets in a rasping wind, while everything inside the barracks is turned upside down. All the furniture is thrown out in the street, our straw-mattresses are shaken empty, and lockers, tables and stools just lay outside in one, big mess. In the evening, everything has to be in tip-top order again and polished bright as a mirror.

On Good Friday, Holy Saturday, and Easter Sunday, from roll call in the morning till late in the evening, more than a thousand clergymen march continuously around the assembly ground in a drizzling and sometimes pouring rain. With not a dry thread on their bodies, they were completely worn-out but mercilessly driven on by the communists. After evening roll call, some priests are forced to climb up on top of six-foot-high cupboards where they have to sing "O Sacred Head, Full of Blood and Wounds."

Together with some Jews, Andreas Rieser, a young Austrian priest, has to clear away old barbed wire fences. He is beaten until he bleeds and then an SS man orders a piece of barbed wire to be plaited into a crown and placed on the man's head. Then he is mocked, spat upon, and beaten, as in the Gospel of Christ's crowning with thorns. Blood-covered and spat upon, he then has to walk around the whole camp: that day was Good Friday!

Far away in the Netherlands, on Good Friday, April 3, 1942, Titus Brandsma is speaking to his fellow prisoners in Barracks IIIA in Camp Amersfoort about "Geert Grote and the Passion of Christ." One of them has drawn a pic-

*ture—Titus Brandsma, seriously wasted and weakened
by dysentery, standing between the wooden bunk beds
where men are sitting and lying, one, two and three high.
He speaks to them about the meaning of suffering. How
can suffering have a role in life? How do you bear it? Titus' words about God's suffering for us and Christ's resur-
rection touch the very core of religious life and are a blessing to the prisoners who must endure the many torments
of life in the camp.*

Apart from all the horrors and torments that we are
exposed to each day, it is always a nerve-racking, killing
thought to be treated as scoundrels and counted as riff-
raff. As the camp commander already told us on the day
of our arrival, we are considered to be the scum and
dregs of the nation. We are expelled from society. We are
treated as slaves and have to perform slave's labor. Neither work nor treatment is human anymore; it is bestial.
Then there is the terrible uncertainty with which we live
continuously: what will happen to me today? What will
happen tomorrow? You are not even sure of the next
hour; even the next minute your life can be at stake. For
the least insignificant thing you can count on a sound
thrashing. You get used to everything, so they say, but it
gnaws away at your nerves. You become completely
numb. In this way, death can mean deliverance. We fear
death no longer, since to die is better than to live.

During my stay in the Admission Block, the block
clerk, an extremely low character in charge of the administration, had assigned me to a very heavy labor
Kommando (work group), namely the *Waffenmeisterei.*
This is a euphemism, no more than an empty word,
hiding some work or other. In this new job of mine, I
have to do very heavy labor at an industrial building site.

All day long I carry bricks in a wheelbarrow, never returning with an empty one, always loaded both with sand or gravel or whatever, and always at double-quick time! Even if you dare to put down the wheelbarrow for only a second, the *Kapo*, the foreman, roars and handles the cudgel. There are eight of us working on a new road. We have a four wheel trolley with less than a wheelbarrow full of gravel on it. However, eight of us cannot move it one inch. We simply lack the strength. But the *Kapo* curses and swears while the SS man is watching. As he rains down strokes of the stick, he keeps on bellowing, "Damn it, they simply will not do it!"

Once you find yourself in a good labor Kommando *where the work is good and the foreman, the* Kapo, *not so cruel, it is most important to hang on as long as possible. However, the job is immediately lost the moment you are admitted to the* Revier *(camp infirmary). So whoever is strong and healthy and therefore seldom or never in the sick barracks, has a good chance to remain in a labor* Kommando *for a long time or even forever.*

Since he is taken to the Revier *quite often because of sickness, weakness and as a guinea pig for medical experiments, Raphael changes work assignments many times. From the heaviest farm work to road sweeper, from mailman to porter on industrial building sites, from carrot scraper to clerk in a forensic biological institution, from house painter to market gardener, in short, he is used for all sorts of things and has to be a jack of all trades.*

If you had been out of a job for a while, you were registered as "unclassified." These inferior unfits have to line up, often for hours, to be selected for another labor *Kommando*. Whenever it enters the mind of the guards, they have to undress and fall in line for "inspection." I have stood for hours and hours, all morning and afternoon, not knowing what would happen and fearing an "Invalid Transport" was about to be composed. In rain or sunshine or stinging cold, those who could not see it through might as well drop dead. The longest time I have ever stood in this "outfit" is on a Sunday afternoon in December from half past twelve till Monday half five in the morning! Hundreds of us are gathered, chilled to the bone, standing and waiting all through the night, until finally the order is issued to get dressed and return to the barracks. Miracle of miracles, I did not even catch a cold!

Another time we stand in the street all morning to be "finished off" with the usual "one, two, three." Hundreds of men have to march past an SS doctor, assisted by some nurses, for selection. Those who get a "one" are still fit for some work or other. Those with "two" are doubtful cases and in need of further examination. Those with "three" are put on transport, which generally means death. The endless row creeps slowly forward until finally our block is called to approach. I have made it a habit never to stand in front in situations of this kind. A wise elder camp inmate once told me that in case the order comes to turn round, which happens sometimes, you would end up as the last person in the row! Whether the guards are getting tired I do not know, but all of a sudden we are making headway, and in less than a minute our group is ready for a "medical" inspection. With my clothes under my arm, I notice the superficial way in which my colleagues are treated but with a fair amount of brutality. I jump towards the doctor together with someone else. While the other stands before him, I sneak off behind his back and disappear into the group "already examined." This way I am safeguarded against "one, two and three!"

You need a sixth sense, as it were, to such dangers, to be capable to discern the signs that intuit the coming of dangerous events. Often it is in the air, although you have no clue what is going on. Close observation and attention, coupled with a large quantity of daring as much as risk, and then, at the critical moment, you have to make yourself "scarce," as we say in camp slang. After that, the best you can do is to "duck" for a couple of hours, since there is often a lot of *antreten* to be heard. It could be something innocent, but you never can tell in advance. It could very well mean the composing of a transport, another labor *Kommando,* or the selection of guinea pigs for all kinds of experiments involving malaria, seawater, phlegmone inflations, etc. To have to make an instantaneous decision without a sound justification could be a matter of really great importance. You let fear, anxiety or sometimes only suspicion do its work. You feel something is up and you thank the Lord every time you get off scotfree. You sense His protection and it is often tangible as well. Especially Blocks 28 and 30, where the clerics live, are dangerous spots, for all *Pfaffen* are death candidates.

Raphael makes friends with Father Henny Zwaans, a Jesuit priest, born in Rotterdam in 1898. He had been arrested on July 26, 1941 in Maastricht, where he was director of a Jesuit college. Zwaans is sentenced to seven months in jail. After six months in Scheveningen he is brought to Kleve, where he is released and arrested anew straight away. In March 1942, he arrives in Dachau

*where he spends a fortnight in the Admission Block. On
Holy Thursday, April 2, he enters Block 28 where Raphael
has been staying for three days. Together, they go through
the last days of Holy Week.*

In those days, Father Henny Zwaans, a Jesuit from
Maastricht, is a terrific support to me. He came to
Block 28 shortly after me and we worked together as
much as possible. He lived for no more than a few
months, but during that short period of time they
managed to make a martyr out of him. Soon Father
Zwaans' health got worse to such a degree that the
twenty minute march to work is extremely hard on
him, partly because of the sore feet each one of us has
from the inferior, ill-fitting shoes. A pair of wooden
sandals, in which we go barefoot, is all we have. Due to
lack of healthy food and care, a wound takes a long
time to heal.

In the morning he is standing next to me at the parade. In a whisper, he prays the prayers of the Holy
Mass to start the day. During the march to work, the
exhausted, emaciated frames have to present the most
disgusting SS songs, sung loud and firm. Those who
do not sing along may count on a blow in the face. Together with the recently ordained Harry Reinders, Father Zwaans and I are employed in the gravel pit. The
gravel has to be scooped up to more than a man's
height, a very straining and fatiguing work. However,
there is a good atmosphere between us. Inconspicuous
we pray the Rosary and the Stations together. Alternating, Father Zwaans and Chaplain Reinders are con-
templating a sacred word without stopping work or
anybody noticing. Yet the *Kapo* has spied on us from
afar and separates us to different places. Shortly after-

wards, Father Zwaans succeeds in returning to the gravel pit and so we continue to help each other as much as we can.

Suddenly, both of us are called to do something else. A wagon filled with bags of cement has to be unloaded. Although a bag weighs only 70 pounds, it is impossible for us to carry one. Each time one bag is put on our shoulders, we almost collapse. I can see that Father Zwaans is unable to hold on much longer so I tell him he should try to get back into the gravel pit before he collapses. But he refuses to leave me. "I will be fine again," he thinks. He is not fine at all and finally I convince him to leave the heavy work. He sneaks behind a wooden cabin near the gravel-pit, but, unfortunately, the *Kapo* sees him and walks up to him. His fist hits Zwaans straight in the face and he falls down to the ground. He must go on working, returning back to the cement. Now two bags are put on his shoulders and he breaks down, much to the amusement of the communists. I pick him up and, when he comes round a bit, we both leave the wagon without paying attention to the others.

Later on, we are in another gravel pit. It is freezing cold. By ten o'clock, I go inside a new factory building where a young man is busy installing glass windowpanes. He has just been given a thick ear by the *Kapo* because he breaks too much glass. I pull myself together and ask the *Kapo* to allow me to cut some glass without breaking it into pieces. He gives me a scornful look, saying, "You are a *Pfaff*, are you not?" I might be a *Pfaff* but I do know how to cut glass! I take a piece of glass and go up and down with the glasscutter quickly. To the *Kapo*'s surprise, every cut is correct and, with my fingers, I break the glass alongside the cuts.

He immediately tells me to stay and work here instead of in the cold gravel pit.

This is such an improvement! I am inside and I do work that I have known for many years. However, Father Zwaans is still outside in the cold. I have to get him inside too. But how? The answer comes to me quickly. A couple of times, the *Kapo* came to take a look and he turns out to be quite satisfied. I tell him that I need someone to knead the putty as the cold makes it almost impossible to work with. "Outside there are plenty who do not know what to do." "Well," he answers, "when you can find one yourself, it is okay with me." I go to Father Zwaans at once and a moment later, he is warming himself a little before he starts kneading the putty. It does not take long for him to try putting in glass panes himself. After a week, he is already quite proficient in the work.

Being hungry all the time is a huge problem. One day, we are together in a large factory hall when a *Kapo* comes towards us to bring us a *Brotzeit*, an extra ration of bread. This is so special, something fantastic. Our joy is indescribable now that we have a bit more to eat than the normal quantity! "The darkest hour is before dawn," Father Zwaans says, and we dispatch our slice of bread with a sincere short prayer. On we go with fresh courage. Now we can stand it much better, that is for sure. So time goes by, one day after the other. At nine, a sign is given to fetch the *Brotzeit*. Standing in long rows, we wait for our extra slice of bread. You should see the shining eyes of the lucky one who gets a *Kante*, the end of the loaf, which is usually a bit thicker. Every crumb of bread is worth gold.

It is not just material things that sustain us. Especially in a place like this, one learns to appreciate the value of spiritual food, be it Holy Communion that can only be received clandestinely on very exceptional occasions or be it conversations through which we try to cheer each other up as much as possible. Father Zwaans says "All in Your honor, Oh Holy Heart of Jesus" every time we work together, and cheerfully, we make another start. However, days spent in bitter cold and draft have broken his weak constitution. In the afternoon, he starts coughing a lot and the dreaded dysentery makes itself felt. It is only a matter of days now before he has to quit working. Also the phlegmones, the open wounds on his feet, make it inevitable that he admit himself to the *Revier*, the camp hospital. A few days later I am taken to the *Revier* myself. We spend a total of three weeks in Block 7, *Stube* 4, a barracks especially for dysentery patients. We speak to each other daily when we are out of our beds to get some fresh air.

By the time the phlegmone wounds are healed to a certain degree, the communist attendants decide that patients can return to their block. They allow us to stay in the *Schonungsblock* during the day. This is considered a great privilege in the eyes of the SS, but in reality it turns out to be an endless torment. We have to stand outside all day, with our half-healed wounds, in rows of ten, or else stay inside a barracks, crammed with a hundred or more in a room that normally houses fifty at the most. Lying down is forbidden; we are ever so happy when the head of the barracks is away and we can lie down on the hard floor. This particular head of the barracks is a first-degree sadist; he beats us and kicks us for no reason at all, irrespective of person, age, or health condition. He seems to prefer sending out the priests to carry the food kettle that weighs about 75 kilos, which is an extremely heavy load for us.

One day, we use the absence of the head of the barracks to lie on the floor, when I see an elderly gentleman holding his hand in his pocket all the time. It is nothing unusual, until I see the crucifix of a rosary sticking out of his pocket. It is clear enough to me now that he is a priest and I crawl towards him. I ask him on which block he belongs. "In Block 26," is his kind answer. So I guessed well. It is a German priest. When I tell him that I am from 28, he is very interested about the situation in our block. Finally, I ask him if he is willing to lend me his rosary for a while. "But of course, be careful that no one sees you." Without anyone noticing, I sneak into a corner and let one bead after the other slide through my fingers. What came over me, now that I could pray a rosary after such a long time, is hard to put into words. I sit on the floor and big tears run down my cheek. I do not know for how long I sat there, but when I crawl back to my friend to return the rosary and to thank him, he says with a laugh, "*Das hättest du auch wohl ohne Träne erledigen konnen!*" No, it was impossible for me to do it without tears, I was moved too much. I was simply too happy.

In the meantime, Titus Brandsma has been taken to Germany. After the terrors of Amersfoort and a short interrogation in Scheveningen, he has arrived in Kleve, a transit prison to Dachau. Although his treatment there is much better, his spiritual needs are increasing. Titus enters into a dark night, full of desperation and despair. He tries to escape from his fate by presenting a petition for internment in a German monastery. Each line reads as a cry of a man in agony of death. "Not my will but Thy will be done..." As he realizes that his road is definitely leading

to Dachau, he is able to accept this and to surrender him-
self to whatever God is asking from him.

The summer months of 1942 are horrible, the worst
in all the years that I have spent in Dachau. Daily men
from our ranks die of hunger and exhaustion. No wonder the first person you see as soon as you have dragged
yourself back to the barracks, dead-tired from work, is
asked "Who died today?" One after the other falls;
death prowls relentlessly and keeps finding new victims. Chaplain Van Rooijen dies on June 16 after Father Zwaans sent him a last blessing from a distance
through the window of the sick barracks. Father Gala-
ma, whom I have heard muttering, "I want all You
want. I want it because You want me to, the way You
want me to, and as long as You want me to," leaves us
on June 20 on an "Invalid" transport, grateful for our
consoling words, but convinced of the fact that it is actually a *Himmelfahrt Kommando* (a work group for as-
cending to heaven). The notice of his death, that we
receive shortly afterwards, says he died on June 20.

More than 900 clerics die in the first eight months of
1942 from hunger and exhaustion, as victims of bio-
chemical experiments, or as guinea pigs. This makes
Dachau into the largest priest cemetery in the world.
On June 19, after a journey from Kleve that lasted six
days, Titus Brandsma arrives in the deepest abyss of mis-
ery named Dachau.

We find ourselves on the parade in the concentration camp in Dachau during evening roll call. A driz-
zly, rainy day is about to end. The sun that has left us
all day, tries for a moment to let its weak rays shine

through the grey leaden clouds. However, it is no longer strong enough to give any color to this dreary day and even less able to provide any warmth. Thousands of dead-tired, hungry looking men fail to notice this last glimpse of sunlight, even though for them it could have been a sign of the ever nearing day of liberation from this hellish place. However, they do not pay any attention at all. They are too tired to even think about it. The day that is just over and the hunger that constricts them all in an iron clasp, deprive many of the power to even turn their heads towards the clouds. The men are lined up in dead-straight rows of ten, beside and behind each other. In that way they form large blocks, each one two meters apart from the next one. A deadly silence hangs over the crowd that, chilled to the bone, is waiting in rain-drenched clothes for the signal that the counting is over with. Even though it is mid-June already, a chilly wind, blowing over the heads and between the rows, makes everyone shiver.

Finally the bawling voice of the SS man on duty barks as a sign that roll call is over. There is a slight commotion in the crowd and a murmuring among the thousands. At a certain moment a lot of eyes turn to the right, where the main entrance of the camp attracts everyone's attention. A group of newcomers, about twenty persons, is being brought in. From a distance, you can easily pick out some priests by their clothing. In a heavy armed convoy they are led away to the Administration Building where all newcomers are "welcomed" before being taken to the so-called *Zugangsblock*. While the gate to freedom shuts down behind those who have just entered, another one opens onto a gloomy, dark and dangerous future. They now are in Dachau!

HEAVEN IS BESIEGED WITH PRAYERS

A few days later I meet Chaplain Rothkrans, who tells me he has seen Father Titus Brandsma in the *Zugangsblock*, the quarantine area for newly arrived prisoners. That is surprising news for me! I have no peace any longer. All I can do is wait for a suitable moment to sneak into the Admission Block. I manage to do this by mixing in with some residents of the block who are being taken inside. Some moments later, I am standing opposite Titus. How thin he has become and how much older he looks in his worn-out prison uniform. He does not recognize me at first as I approach him to greet him. After I tell him who I am, he shakes my hand with sincere warm-heartedness. I ask him how he is doing and he answers, "I am all right, that is to say, rather well, considering the circumstances." Then he asks attentively, "And how about you?" Laughing, I also answer "fairly well under the circumstances" and I take him by the arm to a less conspicuous place where we can exchange a few words. We have to be very careful not to attract the attention of the *Stubenälteste* to avoid any unpleasantness.

The whole situation we are in calls for great cautiousness. That is why our first meeting in the camp can only be a short one. However everything seems to indicate that Father Titus tries to adapt himself to his new environment as much as possible, even though, as he says, it is quite a change. The months he has spent imprisoned have taken a toll. He looks very worn. His stays in various prisons have left unmistakeable marks on his appearance. From behind his thick spectacles, he looks around anxiously and admonishes me to use great caution, since, as he says, I am in forbidden territory. I put his mind at ease and, after exchanging a few more words and wishing him all the best, I go back outside as inconspicuously as possible. From the street, he follows me with his eyes for a few more minutes and calls out that he hopes to come to our block soon, where even more Dutchmen are. For us who are in Block 28, it is only a matter of patient waiting until this will happen.

Block 28, together with 26 and 30, is one of the last three barracks on the left hand side of the main street of the camp. They are known as Pfarrerblöcke, *the priests' barracks. The priests' barracks are separated from the other barracks by barbed wire, so great was the Nazi fear of the influence of religion. About 2600 Protestant and Catholic clergy are living in this "camp within the camp" by the time Titus Brandsma arrives there. This immense community is made up of different nationalities. Where in the world can one find a religious community or a monastery where the Church is represented by such "catholicity"? Here, almost every rank of the church hierarchy is hiding underneath the "zebra" uniform. A Polish bishop, Msgr. Kozal, dies in 1942 after a long agony. There is a French abbot and in 1944 another French bishop, Msgr. Gabriel Piquet of Clermont-Ferrand, arrives. Further, there are vicar-generals, deans, four with the title of archdeacon, pastors, chaplains, students-priests and brothers. There are 39 different Orders and Congregations represented in all (the Polish clergy not included). Among them are the Jesuits with 26 members, then the Benedictines with 17, and the Franciscans and Pallottines with 11 members each. There are also Capuchins, Carmelites, Dominicans, Redemptorists, Au-*

gustinians, Assumptionists, Salvatorians, Norbertines, Trappists, Missionaries of the Divine Word, Servites, Lazarists and members of many other Orders and Congregations. The numbers climb steadily as the day of liberation approaches.

When Titus Brandsma is transferred from the Admission Block to Block 28 at the end of June 1942, he ends up in this motley mixture of servants of God's Church, where one cannot tell the one from the other by outward appearance.

As soon as we see Titus, he is immediately surrounded by a group of Dutchmen greeting him. Of course they ask him how he is doing and how it has gone in the Admission Block, since everyone knows from firsthand experience what a difficult initiation this is for every newcomer. His spontaneous reaction is, "Thank God, I am out of that hell! That was no life there. At least I am with all of you now!" He says this with a sigh of relief, but nevertheless we have to laugh and try to make it clear to him that the real Dachau life is just beginning. "Whatever it may be like, I will do my best not to make things too difficult for the gentlemen and to attract as little attention as possible," he says.

Together we walk in the direction of *Stube III*, the living quarters where he will be registered. With two other newcomers who have arrived together with Titus, the Jesuit Leon de Coninck and Pastor Lamboray from Belgium, he enters the barracks, where *Stubenälteste* Walter Thiel receives them. After the block clerk is finished, each receives a food bowl, mug, plate, knife, and spoon. The *Spindl*, the locker where they can put dinner things, is pointed out to them and they are told where to find their beds in the dormitory. The

Stubenälteste emphasizes that he requires a religious observance of rules and prescriptions, and stresses the necessity of preserving order. Then, he continues, one can have a good time with him!

While he is still fascinating the newcomers with a flow of words, the block warden enters the room. He has a stick in his hand, as usual. Immediately he starts to yell and lash out like a madman, so that everyone runs for cover. He begins to fire off a speech to the newcomers about *Sauberkeit und Ordnung* (cleanliness and order), using a lot of strong language, and then ends in a roar, "So, now you know what to expect here. You can be sure that I will bring you to your knees!" Finally, after turning around with one more furious glare, he goes back outside.

The name of this head of the barracks is Fritz Becher, a prisoner like us, however, strong and well fed at the cost of others. He used to be a member of the SA, but was punished because of a number of crimes and sent to a concentration camp. He is a real criminal; rudeness and uncontrolled action are written on his face. The prisoners who are his subjects are continuously exposed to the coarsest of brutalities. He treats priests, in particular, in an unscrupulous and unprincipled manner and bears a big hatred against them, which he openly admits. He never has a kind word for one of us; to him we are papists, bandits and agitators, as he states in his speeches from time after time. Not a day passes without a beating. He treats each of us like dogs. It is impossible to enter the room without a beating and scolding from him. Often he beats someone or another till he bleeds, for no reason at all.

It is a real disillusionment for Titus to get to know such a brute, and he does his utmost to stay away from him as much as possible. He cannot understand how a human being can act like that. Not only the *Blockälteste* but also the *Stubenälteste* become outraged quite often, wielding the stick exorbitantly. They hit us wherever they can, swinging wildly with or without reason, always accompanied by a stream of curses and abusive language. Titus really does his best to carry out, as well as possible, all that he is given to do. Yet sometimes his age and especially his failing health play a trick on him. Because of this, he is not always that fast. Since he wants to do things so precisely, he often draws the attention of the *Stubenälteste*, which once again means a blow with a fist or a stick.

Titus is always the personification of calm and composure when it comes to getting along with others, even when the *Blockälteste* or *Stubenälteste* beats him up. Afterwards, he would not even curse them or call them names like *Bochen*. There is no discernable sign of hatred or aversion toward the Nazis or guards or those who beat or maltreat him. When he is asked why he got beaten, "Oh, it is all over now," is all he says. He even keeps speaking with the *Blockälteste* and *Stubenälteste* in his own friendly way. It always draws our attention because the reason for them to call you is often to account for some sort of "crime." Apart from that, you would rather keep out of their way as far and as much as possible. But Titus, with his natural kindness, still tries to make some kind of connection with them by talking. Most of the time, the conversation ends with a kick or a cuff around his ears, but that does not stop him from being friendly with them. I can still hear the bellowing voice of the *Blockälteste*, "Get out of here, you bumbling idiot!" Once after such an occasion, I tell Titus, "By all means, stop talking with those guys. You will not get anywhere with them. At best, you will get a thrashing." But then he would answer, "That is no reason to stop talking with them. Who knows? Maybe something will stick."

"One must pray for these people," I hear him say frequently, "so that they will see the light."

The moment Titus joins us in Block 28, he is assigned to a labor *Kommando* called *Liebhof* (garden of love). This is a farm surrounded by several hectares of land. The majority of people at work here are priests, about a hundred in all. Every day he marches there in his uncomfortable, clumsy soldiers' boots that are much too big for him. Singing along, the column marches out of the camp, crosses Eicke-Platz and continues past the villas of the guards, which have been built by prisoners on both sides of the broad *Straße der SS* (SS Street). After a march of roughly half an hour by a roundabout way between barracks and warehouses, one reaches *Liebhof.*

A field cross stands in a bend of the road. For many prisoners, especially the priests, it is a mystery why this cross has never been removed by the Nazis. Apparently the cross has been at that place for years without any maintenance. Anyway, it is leaning to one side, pushed over by the low-hanging branches of a tree. Many must have stolen a silent glance at the Crucified, while they pass by singing. There is no doubt at all that Titus, too, has greeted the Cross as he passed by, which would have awakened in him one more thought of fresh courage.

Among the SS that escort the prisoners are many who hate God and religion openly. There is, for instance, a young SS guard, who cannot stand the sight of that cross. Each time the column marches past it, he kicks it as he passes by. The cross shakes under the rough kick from the boot of this strongly built SS man. Among prisoners he has acquired the nickname *Kulturträger*, mainly because of the way he acts and the stupid things he reels off all the time. So it is always a real satisfaction to him any time he can give the cross a good kick.

One day, however, when we are on our way to the *Liebhof,* passing this place, a young man suddenly jumps out of the row towards the cross. He has hidden several blocks of wood underneath his jacket and starts to hammer them powerfully into the ground, one after the other, beside the pedestal of the cross. The *Kulturträger* instantly understands what is going on and bellows a long drawn-out "*Haaalt!*" as if it is the end of the world. All of us freeze on the spot. SS and prisoners stare, frozen, at the man under the cross. Leaving the row is regarded as a *Fluchtversuch*, attempted escape. In such a case, every SS is under orders to shoot immediately. If he makes a hit, and there is one prisoner less to report when they return in the camp that evening, he gets a reward of twenty marks and fourteen days extra leave. Now is another chance for such a special piece of luck. Immediately, all SS men take aim at the man who is still working, but no one lets a shot loose. Already he has the first log secure in the marshy ground when the *Kulturträger* jumps at him fuming and fretting, shouting, "Back, back, you pig! I am going to shoot you to pieces!" He throws himself upon the young prisoner, ready to kick him. But the latter stands proud and upright in front of him, saying with a loud voice "Nobody is allowed to disgrace the cross in my presence!" The *Kulturträger* is beyond speech. He turns to the leader of the *Kommando* and says, "Commandant, this is out-right rebellion!" A deep silence hangs in the air, only broken by the voice of the young man with the words, "I am a Christian and will not let the cross be maligned." The *Kulturträger*, hissing angrily through his teeth, grabs his gun once more and points, as if he wants to shoot him down. At that moment the commander orders to move on, while he speaks to the young man, "Get going now. We will talk about this later!"

The atmosphere among the prisoners is tense the whole day, in expectation of what will happen next. After being questioned by the commander, the young man is presented to the *Lagerführer*, who asks him what he does for a living. "Theology student in the Society of Jesus," he answers. At these words, the SS man straightens his shoulders and is silent. "You are aware of the fact that rebellion carries the death penalty, are you not? It would be a shame for you to die for such a stupid thing," he says to the student.

That evening, when we all return to the barracks, the student is stopped at the entrance of the camp and brought before the *Lagerführer*. In the priest block prayers are offered for him. Some even pray the prayers for the dying. Nobody expects to see him alive ever again. All of a sudden the door of the room swings open and the student walks in, laughing. Hundreds of pair of eyes turns towards him in amazement. He is bombarded with questions and has to relate how everything has turned out. "Oh," he says, "the *Lagerführer* wanted to know exactly what was going on. Then I told him everything. After that, the *Kulturträger* was sent out of the room and we were alone. Then I told him convincingly that we Christians have to defend the cross with our lives. He listened with close attention. At the end of my account, he said to me: "Do not let it ever happen again, understand? Tomorrow take two men with you. See that you get proper tools and material and a guard. The cross has to be repaired!" The cross is still standing there! Restored and in the same place, it has survived *das Tausendjährige Reich* (the thousand year Reich)!

At every work project, a *Kapo* is in charge, together with his assistant, the *Subkapo*. Adolf Zuleger is the *Kapo* that sways the sceptre at the *Liebhof* during the time that Titus works there. He is too stupid for words and has no notion of farm work either. He does not know the difference between rye and oats, for example. He is a professional fireman, but is much better at yelling, kicking, and beating. It is amazing to learn where he gets all the rough words he uses. His assistant, Hermann, is a Communist like his master. Sometimes he is even better at brutalizing than Adolf. His abusing and beating is a matter of force of habit. You might as well get used to it, or even better ignore it, when he starts to reel off a stream of curses over the prisoners' heads once again.

The primary work, especially in the summertime, is to weed, weed, and weed some more. All those herbs like basil, savory, kummel, marjoram, thyme and whatever else their names might be, need to be weeded regularly, so that there are absolutely no weeds left in the beds. On closer inspection, this work is not so heavy, but the circumstances make it very hard. First of all, there are the long, long hours in all sorts of weather conditions, either bent over or squatted down. In the summer the scorching sun burns down on you, and when it rains, you spend the whole day in the field in clothes that are soaking wet. Add to that the never ending gnawing hunger. To stop working because of rain or thunder is out of the question. The very cold and wet spring of 1942 makes many victims in this field. That is why the prisoners change the name of *Liebhof* into *Friedhof* (cemetery). In the evening, the exhausted, tormented prisoners drag themselves back to the camp. It often happens that Titus is so tired that he can hardly stand or walk. The two Polish Carmelites who also work at the *Liebhof*, Hilarius Januzewski, prior of the Carmelite monastery in Krakow, and Albertus Urbanski, take him between them and support him on the way back to the camp. They help Titus a lot and do all they can to lighten his suffering.

As soon as Titus is assigned to a work *Kommando* outside the camp, he is allowed to change his wooden slippers for a pair of heavy shoes with wooden soles and hard leather covering. Although this could sometimes be a real improvement, for Titus those shoes were the primary reason that he ruins his feet. The shoes are way too big and they rub his feet raw. Because of a lack of good nursing care, they do not heal (or only heal with difficulty). In the beginning, it is only a couple of insignificant little scrapes, but gradually these get worse and become big festering sores, the so-called phlegmones that gnaw away the flesh down to the bone and cause terrible pain. No one is allowed to bandage his own wounds. You have to go to the camp hospital that offers the possibility two or three times a week to have any wounds bandaged. Many prefer not to go, since the treatment there is so bad and, more than anything else, so rough. None of the "nurses" that you meet there are trained to care for the

sick or to treat them. Only a butcher, a blacksmith, a
field worker or some such layperson is hidden under
the white jackets. Personally, I have witnessed opera-
tions without any anaesthetics and the unnecessary
amputation of limbs, that is to say, that a skillful treatment could very well have prevented the amputation.

Nonetheless, the so-called "bandage hour" is frequently used. The most that you get there is a little
salve and a bandage, a kick in the pants and then immediately *der Nächste* (the next) is called. Given such a
"loving" treatment, I have torn a towel in two pieces
that serve well to bind Titus' wounds. The festering
wounds on his feet are about 2 to 3 inches long. Putting
on or taking off of the heavy shoes especially causes him
much pain. Sometimes we go outside together and sit
on the sidewalk, since there is no space inside. During
the treatment, Titus makes sure that none of the block
personnel sees us. Carefully, I take his shoes off, wipe
the pus out of the wounds with a little piece of clean
paper, and then wrap a piece of the towel around his
foot. It takes some effort to get his feet back in the
shoes again, but eventually he succeeds. I can tell by his
face that I have caused him a lot of pain, but after I help
him get back on his feet, he gives me a pat on the shoulder, smiles a little and says, "There you are, my dear
brother, now I am back to being a real gentleman." He
takes the first steps gingerly, but then, in spite of all the
pain, he just goes on his way. You can see that he has to
conquer himself, so that, in spite of everything, nothing
would be noticed. He is always grateful for everything
that anyone does for him, even the smallest things. He
does not talk about the pain or the sickness that he has
to endure, but he accepts everything with a patience
that we not only notice but also admire, and which

makes a deep impression on all of us. Titus has a similar attitude towards the food. The spectre of hunger is with us day and night and for many it is a real obsession to talk about food all the time. The most delicious dishes and exquisite menus spring from the imaginative minds of starving men. As a consequence, the hunger is felt even more, only to find out in the end that it is all an illusion.

Hunger! Have you got any idea what that means? I venture to say that what you call "hunger" is "appetite" at the most! However, in the camp there is real famine. Not only are we given little food, but it is also bad. The amount of food that is rationed out in 1942 consists of 200 to 250 grams of bread in the evening and, in the afternoon, some warm water in which a few cabbage leaves or pieces of beet are floating. Twice a week, we get two *Pellkartoffeln* (jacket-boiled potatoes). It is better to eat the scanty bread ration at once, but it is meant to serve the next day. If you divide it into portions, to eat some in the evening and the rest during the next day, it is too little to get a sense of having had some kind of a meal, both in the evening as well as the next morning. No need to say that the food is not doing us much good. Our bodyweight goes down rapidly. In three months time, I have lost 30 kilos, and the food we get is not enough to get me back to my normal weight again. This is true for most of us. We are starving. Only the Communist staff, the *Blockälteste* and *Stubenältesten*, look much better, thanks to the food they withhold from us. There is only one thought on our minds: food! The eyes of the prisoners continually wander in order to look for food: crusts of bread, carrots or beets. We even look for edible remnants in garbage cans.

Titus manages to control himself exceptionally well. There is no doubt that he feels the hunger as much as anyone else. Not only the hard work he has to do but also malnutrition reduce his strength very rapidly. He often says to me, "Who could ever have imagined that we could dine so splendidly on a piece of bread and a couple of *Pellmänner*, his word for the jacket-boiled potatoes. "Let us be grateful to the good Lord," he says. "Things could be worse."

So life for the clerics in 1942 is extremely tough. Work lasts from morning till evening and the ravenous hunger is an everlasting torment. Even worse is the nerve-wracking rush in which the day's work has to be done, as well as the senseless, unnecessary things that make work so much more difficult. It starts in the morning when we get up. The short sleep is often accompanied by dreams. The continuous hunger teases our imagination with pictures of plenty of tasty food, and conversations about food often fill the day, as I said before. Or you dream of home in the Netherlands, of confreres, and of family. Then, all of a sudden this dream world is cruelly driven from you by the growling of the "bear," the claxon that gives the wake-up signal at four in the morning. A new day is about to begin. Whatever is left of the peaceful sense of sleep is driven away by the most important ceremony, the *tadellos*, making of the beds (the word *tadellos*, "faultless," is always on the lips of the *Stubenälteste*). With a certain routine that everyone has grown into, we are busy to have it end as quick as possible. Unfortunately, we Dutch have a bad name with the *Stubenälteste* in general. Our reputation in *Bettenbau* is not in high favor with the people. Luckily, I can touch the ceiling of the dormitory with my nose, three beds high, and I am always done with the "cigar box" quickly. Most often, I have finished before Titus, whose bed is in the bottom row and I am able to help him for a few moments. In this way, everything is done before the *Stubenälteste* arrives for inspection. He enters with a stick in his hand and violently chases all who are not yet ready out of the room. This happens especially to the elderly and those who are rather slow and not very sharp.

In the meantime, during the nervous bustle in the dormitory, when the beds are made, some of us have gone to the kitchen to get the coffee. This is one of the hardest chores within the camp. The *Kubel*, a large double walled thermos kettle, weighs nearly 40 kilos when empty. Add to that the same amount of litres of coffee or soup and the weight increases to more than 75 kilos. Two of us have to carry the kettle, which is almost impossible. There is no mercy nor excuse; everybody has to perform this heavy task in turn.

Often Titus and I have lugged about a kettle, but already after a few steps we had to put it down and take a rest. However, that luxury is not always granted, especially when someone of the block's staff is escorting. He keeps you going by beating, kicking, and strong language. Dead tired, one arrives in the barracks, often too tired to move a foot.

Eating, gulping down some coffee, and washing up the bowl, everything happens in a rush, because all jostle at the water taps. Then you use a piece of paper to make the bowl as smooth as a mirror. I usually grab Titus' plate to do the washing up, since he is often not quick enough to do it, and then I am back in the room before *Stubendienst* is called out. This means that all of us leave the room in a rush because it is going to be put to rights and scrubbed.

One morning, after we have all been chased outside, I see Titus coming towards me without his glasses on. It turns out that he has forgotten them; they are still in his locker. He wants to go back immediately and get his glasses, but I keep him from doing this, saying it is already *Stubendienst*, and he is not allowed to go back into the room. I suggest that I slip back in inconspicuously and get his glasses from his locker. However, he will hear nothing of the kind, since it is strictly forbidden to touch another man's locker. This is immediately regarded as an attempt to steal. Before we can discuss it further, he has already stepped back into the room and has quickly gone to his locker. The door of his locker squeaks as he opens it, which attracts the attention of the *Stubenälteste*. As he turns around, he sees Titus and shouts at him, "What is going on?" "I have forgotten my glasses, *Herr Stubenälteste*" is Titus' polite answer. Yet before he has reached the door, the sadist's club strikes down upon the innocent Titus. "I will teach you to forget," he yells continually. One forceful whack with the stick and the glasses fly past, landing in pieces on the street. Blow after blow comes down on Titus' head so that he falls straight to the ground. I can still hear the *Stubenälteste* screaming. When he has finally had enough of his brutal behavior, Titus scrambles to his feet and stands in front of me, bleeding from his nose and mouth, but without his glasses. I pick up the pieces and ask him if it hurts, but he does not take it seriously at all. He just answers, "Nothing at all, my dear brother. Otherwise, you would have been beaten up." Our fellow countrymen immediately surround us, and we count no less than 17 drops of blood on his jacket. The Dutchmen ask what has happened but Titus does not think it is worth talking about. He wants to forget and forgive everything right away.

A few moments later, the command *antreten* – falling in line for general roll call – is already echoing. All residents of the block have to line up in rows of ten. The smallest men are first in line for the march to the parade and the bigger ones are behind them. Titus' place is in the second row from the front while mine is in the next to the last row of the column. Everyone has to march exactly in step, always paying attention to the people who are on their right and their left. Singing a soldier's song, the column then proceeds to the roll call in military paces. This march is a real martyrdom for many, even though it is no more than 700 meters from Block 28 to the assembly ground. This goes for Titus, too, who has the most serious wounds on his feet.

Once we arrive at the parade, the various blocks take up their positions next to each other. Then there is a wait for the *Rapportführer*, who has to give the final count of the prisoners present to the camp commander. In general, the clergy use this time of waiting in the fresh early hour of the morning for a short but ardent prayer. This is the only time in the day when you have a few minutes to peacefully direct your thoughts to Him who is the Father of all and who does not forget us, even in the severest and most difficult times. A short meditation or a decade of the rosary, prayed in silence, fill the few minutes before the beginning of the roll call. Then Heaven is besieged with prayers for strength from the good Lord for the day to come.

While we stand there we are often struck by the splendid colors of the rising sun. The horizon glows in the most divergent shades of golden yellow and vermilion, which then turn into a deep purple, and a glorious ultramarine. Those incredibly beautiful morning skies often catch the attention of all of us there. I do not think any painter has enough colors on his palette to be able to re-produce such a prodigy of nature with his brush. Such a sublime spectacle of nature can direct your thoughts for a few moments towards Him, the Creator of the universe, whose power and majesty know no boundaries.

Most of the time, morning roll call goes pretty fast, since we have to go to work immediately afterwards. But in the evening, when we have returned to camp af-ter work, dead tired, it can sometimes take hours be-fore the SS will condescend to take the roll. Once dur-ing evening roll call, when attention to the different heights of the prisoners is less strict, I stand next to Ti-tus. There seems to be no end to the waiting and we only stay on our feet with difficulty. In passing, I say to Titus, "How long have we been standing here? What are we waiting for this time?' Laconically, he replies, "Oh, my dear brother, let us have a little patience and wait. After all, we have the time." He is and remains the personification of calm and composure.

Even this terrible ceremony, roll call, comes to an end and finally we are dismissed. The lay prisoners are allowed to eat, but the clergy, because they are clergy, have to do some extra marching and singing under the direction of the staff of the block and *Stubenälteste* Becker yelling his orders. For twenty minutes, he makes us march up and down the main street. Often we have to run up and down to get us even more tired. With a devilish grin on his face, Becker stands on the sidewalk, watching together with the rest of the block personnel. So many have fallen down, but Becker, roughly, puts them back on their feet. I can still see Ti-tus stumble between the rows, since they do not leave

him in peace either, although he is close to exhaustion.
Then finally we are allowed to turn in the barracks.

Before we can eat our meal, we have to polish our
shoes, that is to say, wash. Then there is the strict rule
that everyone should wash his feet before going to bed.
We all have to present our feet to the *Stubenälteste* who
checks if they are really clean. Now considering the fact
that everybody tries to get into the washing room to
have a wash at the same time, the floor soon turns into a
dirty mess; all of us walk in the spilled water. Then, after
having washed your feet, you have to return to the dormitory barefoot. No wonder that the feet get dirty again
in such chaos! So it can easily happen that you are
caught with "dirty feet." That is a good enough reason
to start another scuffle and slugging match. You pass the
inspection with trembling legs, happy and glad when
you get permission to enter the dormitory to seek your
bed, even if it is under the yelling and raging voice of the
Stubenälteste. Some "chosen ones" have to scrub the
floor for the third time and arrange all the shoes in the
racks in a row, although they are jaded like the rest of us.
In this way, even cleanliness and order become martyrdom for many of us. The rest of us get to bed and sink
in a deep sleep in no time.

On Sundays and holidays, we have to work just as
well, at least before 1943. Later, things are softened,
and working on Sunday is abolished for most of the labor *Kommandos*. However, do not think for one moment that such a holiday means you have nothing to
do. Often, life in the barracks is even more difficult
than a normal working day. The block personnel are incredibly creative when it comes to forcing all kind of
activities upon us, especially when it concerns the
cleaning of living rooms and dormitories. Often one

can find Titus standing on the windowsill, polishing the window panes with a ball of paper. Not even the mark of a fly is to be discovered on it. So he stands there for hours at a stretch and breaths against the glass, rubbing as if he has never done anything else in his life. Such a task is given to a university professor, who gave lectures on the history of mysticism and other profound subjects only a few months ago! Yet he does this humble, obtuse work with as much dedication as he used to initiate his students in philosophy. When he has to work with the "Blocker," the scrubber, which is obviously too hard for him, it does not take long before the *Stubenälteste* starts to beat his weakened, emaciated body, because the work is not going fast enough. You can never do any good in the eyes of the *Stubenälteste*. For no reason at all, he starts to act like a madman, raving and raging. Titus is an easy victim for him. His wisdom is no match to such absurdity.

The love for suffering, which Titus admires so much in the saints of our Order and in the stigmatised he loves to speak about, is really growing in him to the degree of heroism. To become one with the Passion of Christ, he gladly bears all pains and accepts the torments he has to endure with great joy. How often I have seen the head of the barracks throw himself angrily upon Titus and beat him unmercifully. One blow from his powerful fist is enough to make Titus hit the ground, and when he is asked afterwards why he was beaten, the answer is always the same, "Oh, never mind. It is not so bad. I have already forgotten it." He would never speak of them in offensive words, but he did urge us to pray for them. One time, I asked him what he thinks of when he is beaten and he admitted that his prayer is always, "Lord, forgive him!"

In all his pain, he must have kept his eyes on the suffering Christ, for where else could he find the strength to bear all this with so much calmness?

It is strictly forbidden to make any religious sign or gesture. Making the sign of the cross is enough to get you a slap in the face. Even so, I often see Titus praying and sometimes we have to remind him not to be so conspicuous, in order to avoid attracting the attention of the block personnel and giving them an opportunity to strike or curse him. "Come, let us go outside then," he says, and he asks me to pray that beautiful little prayer to Mary that he no longer knows completely by heart. Walking beside him, I quietly pray the following little prayer aloud:

> Most blessed and immaculate Virgin, the glory and splendor of Carmel, who looks with special favor upon all who wear your venerable cloth, look mercifully on me too and cover me with the mantel of your motherly protection. Strengthen my weakness with your strength. Lighten the darkness of my heart with your wisdom. Increase faith, hope, and love in me. Adorn my soul with graces and virtues to such an extent that it may always be well beloved by you and your divine Son. Assist me during my life, comfort me in the hour of death with your loving presence, and present me to the Most Holy Trinity as your child and servant so that I may glorify and praise you forever. Amen.

"Yes, my dear brother," he would say, "Mary has to stand by us and help us. If she stretches out her hand over us, we can bear a lot." Every morning, we walk up and down the street between the blocks. When the "bear" growled, Titus often said, "Now, let us begin the new day with fresh courage." With a laugh he would add, "In two months time we will all be back home!" In such a way, he tried to bolster the courage of everyone who listened to him time and time again, for "courage lost is everything lost." That was his motto.

Among the Polish priests is a secular priest from a parish where a Carmelite monastery used to be. He talks about it now and then and wants to hear more and more about our Order from Titus. One day, he utters his desire to be admitted to the Third Order of Carmel. He had already started the necessary novitiate in Poland, but was arrested before he could make his profession. He fears never to return to his fatherland. That is why Titus decides to take Thaddeus' (that is his Christian name) vows, after a preceding conference and a communal novena in honor of Our Lady of Mount Carmel. It all happens very inconspicuously, without any solemn ceremony, amidst the many who walk in the street. It is July 16, 1942, the feast of Our Lady of Mount Carmel. Titus lays his hands on him and puts him under the special protection of Mary, while John of the Cross – his name from now on – promises to repeat everything in a solemn and official manner, if he might ever return in Poland alive. In this way, Titus practices spiritual care even inside the camp, despite the threat of severe punishments.

It most certainly is a pleasure for Titus to be surrounded by a number of countrymen. There are the secular priests Jansen, Keuler, Kuyper, Lemmens, Van Lierop, Rothkrans and Wuyster and the religious priests Van Genuchten, O.F.M., Van Gestel, S.J., Othmarus Lips, O.F.M. Cap., the Augustinian Christoph Vasen and Henny Zwaans, S.J. There are also some vicars with whom he has a friendly association. Last, but not least, there is the Rev. J. Kaptein. The trip to Dachau, a journey they made together, has been the start of a warm contact between them. It is always a great pleasure for Titus to speak of Mary in a circle of confreres. He likes to fill the rare, unobserved moments with some kind of religious conversation or to listen attentively to one of the other Dutch clergy speaking an edifying word. Despite his erudition, he is very modest. He will never push himself in the foreground or force his opinion upon others. In the few spare minutes before morning roll call, one can often see Titus in such a circle of good friends. Almost every morning he finds the time for a spiritual moment speaking either of Mary or of Teresa of Avila who has been his favorite study and meditation subject all his life. Then his thoughts go out to his future plans: to publish a biography of Father Brugman or Teresa. The first chapters on her life were already written during the first months of his imprisonment. This is what he talks about being amongst his friends, exchanging ideas and opinions with enthusiasm.

Even though the company of all these friends is certainly a support for Titus, none of them can prevent his health from visibly falling off. His ravaged body is like a fragile vessel that you are afraid to touch for fear of breaking it. Such a weak constitution still has to perform heavy labor, march long distances, stand for hours at a time on the assembly ground and endure all sorts of harassing and mistreatment. Yet he always finds his strength and resilience in God.

As later revealed, he never hints at all about the misery he experiences in his letters home. It is always "I am fine!" Once he added "You have to adapt yourself to new situations, and with God's help that works here too. Our dear Lord will keep on helping us!" Does not a tremendous confidence in God resound in such words? Do not these words describe him to the full? In the midst of all the troubles and misery, hunger, and pain, he pays no attention at all to himself and just places a great confidence in God. That is why he can also calmly say, "I am fine!' He knows he is in the fatherly hand of God to whom he completely surrenders himself in a childlike simplicity of heart. May all who find themselves in difficult situations direct all their confidence to the good Lord in order to find the strength and courage they need to persevere and not just collapse under it. How often has he told those who came in contact with him, "Leave that up to the Lord. Do your best and God will do the rest!" This is no hollow catch phrase; it is his holy conviction. We see in him an example, and in this way he becomes an encouragement for us to persevere in all the many difficult hours. He knows how to give fresh courage to someone by pointing to our good Father in Heaven.

Never a cutting word comes from his lips and he would never laugh if someone were to speak such words. In his social interactions, he is never haughty. He talks with everyone, without lording his learning over them. He can be described as being as "simple as a dove." The slyness of a snake is completely strange to him. His sole point of perspective is God and it takes little effort for him to adjust to very different people and very hard situations. In his childlike simplicity and spontaneous way of associating, he is attractive to all.

In January 1941, a primitive chapel was erected in Block 26, the barracks of the German priests. By removing a wall between a living quarter and a dormitory, a large room was created where Holy Mass is celebrated every morning before the rest of the camp is awake. From our block street (between 26 and 28), in the early morning hour, we can clearly see the flickering lights of the candles on the altar through the white-painted windows of the chapel. Often I stand still for a few moments together with Titus and, in thought, we dwell on the Holy Sacrifice that we cannot attend in the flesh. It is not long before head of the barracks Becker comes running outside and chases us away.

I have an appointment with a German priest, a Richard Schneider, whom I work with at the Plantage. He promises to bring the Holy Communion to me from time to time as long as I keep quiet about it. The next morning, while thousands of us are gathered at the parade, I keep looking to the left where the clergy of Block 26 are lined up. At a given moment Richard looks to the side and our eyes meet. With a slight nod he acknowledges that I should try and meet him in a few minutes. After roll call is over and the order "formation of labor commands" is issued, everyone goes to the place where his work group is lined up. In the busy coming and going of all these people, it is easy for me to approach Richard unnoticed. Without stopping and also without saying a word, he hands a small piece of white paper that hides the host inconspicuously. I cannot help trembling for holy joy now that I may receive this precious treasure in person for the first time. Beforehand I had torn a piece of lining in the hem of my trousers, underneath the belt that I wear around my waist, and that is where I hide the Holy Species. More than happy, I go to Father Titus, beckon him aside and once we think nobody is spying on us, I carefully hand over the host to him. He rejoices as much as I do that I have succeeded in accomplishing this task. In turn, he hides it under the wash-leather that is in his case for his glasses. As a precaution, we agree to communicate that afternoon after we have returned from work. It is hard to find words that express the joy this meant to both of us. After a long time, Our Savior is so near to us. He has followed us into our confinement and, as a prisoner Himself, He wants to strengthen us in all the vicissitudes and perils that we are exposed to any time of the day.

Back in the barracks, with a few moments off after our scarce dinner, we walk up and down the block street several times. Titus speaks some pious words of faith and love for Christ in the Holy Sacrament. Having done our communal preparations, Titus looks around carefully to see that nobody is watching us. When he is convinced that there is no danger, he gives Holy Communion to me. Then we both go our way, with Christ in our heart, praying amidst the many other prisoners who have gradually come outside. Nobody has noticed anything but we are supremely happy. We have often said to each other, "Who would have ever believed or dared to expect that we could receive communion even inside the camp!" Often, he breaks the Holy Communion in two. One part is for communion with our Dutch confreres, sometimes up to ten persons. The other part is for me to keep. In the evening, when we are back in the barracks again, I give it back to him and he keeps it underneath the wash-leather in his glass case.

If the bodily hunger is terrible, the spiritual hunger is even worse. Whenever we happen to have the good fortune to receive communion, we feel interiorly strengthened and we can bear everything much better. Titus often says that, according to the great St. Teresa, Eucharist is not only spiritual food, but it also strengthens the body. Indeed, many of us experience this. A consuming homesickness for the Church's channels of grace burns within us. I learn to appreciate then rightly and for their true value in the desolation of Dachau's exile. Even though we who live in Block 28 are not allowed to enter the chapel, no one can prevent the hidden God-man from coming to us.

As we prepare ourselves for Holy Communion together in the camp street, Titus often speaks of the "Great Prisoner" Christ in the Blessed Sacrament. He points out to me how Christ Himself has been a prisoner and how he has endured so much mockery and derision, flagellation, the crowning with thorns, and the crucifixion simply out of love for us, and that we have to bear our imprisonment for love of Him. "Above all, let us not forget this whenever something painful happens to us here. We have to use that moment to respond to his love. How trivial is everything that we experience here in comparison with what he has suffered for us," he tells me.

One evening, without anybody else seeing, I give the host to Titus. Evening roll call is over and everyone tries to eat as quickly as possible and to wash their feet, so that they can lay their tired limbs to rest. Before we get that far, we first have to go by the *Stubenälteste*, not only for the feet inspection, but also for a body search, to see if we are carrying anything on our bodies. It is strictly forbidden to take anything with you into the dormitory. It is not even allowed us to eat a piece of bread quietly in bed. Nor is it permitted to take care of your wounds— a good reason for one to have gladly smuggled a piece of cloth into the dormitory. The *Stubenälteste* probes all of us from top to bottom, including our feet.

That evening in question, I am fortunate enough to pass the inspection and I go into the dormitory. As soon as I enter the room I see that Titus is not yet in bed. Suddenly I hear the bawling voice of the *Stubenälteste* behind me, "Ah, Brandsma, you dirty pig." Terrified, I look around and see Titus standing before the one in charge of the room while he checks up on his feet. Titus has just come out of the washroom, and has presumably dirtied the soles of his feet a little on the way back to the dormitory. Along with several others, he is put to one side, and they have to wait till the rest are in bed. I continue watching from the dormitory to see what else is going to happen. After a few minutes I hear the *Stubenälteste* hollering over and over again, "I will teach you how to keep clean!" Immediately, he deals out blows to all those who are standing nearest to him. I shudder at the thought of Titus receiving such a treatment too, for only a few minutes before I have given him the host that he keeps in the eyeglass case hidden under his armpit. If it is discovered, the consequences can only be guessed at. When it is Titus' turn, the *Stubenälteste* shouts, "Are you a filthy bastard too?" hitting him at the same time with his club, so that Titus tumbles on the floor in one blow. The man's anger knows no bounds. He beats and kicks Titus wherever he can, so that he rolls all over the ground. Crawling, he tries to reach the threshold of the dormitory, but before he can make it, he has to pay an unmerciful price. All the time, I hear him bellowing loudly, as only these guys do. Finally, Titus manages to drag his sore body over the threshold into the dormitory. Seeing this, I lift him up, lead him to his bed and cover him up as well as I can, while asking him if he is in a lot of pain. However, Titus wants no word of comfort. Smiling, he looks at me and whispers, "Oh, my dear brother, I knew whom I was carrying with me!" Saying this, he points to the eyeglass case that he holds cautiously pressed against his body under his left arm. I just stand beside him for a moment and then he says, "Come, let us pray an *Adoro Te* together." I want to sink down on my knees, but he is afraid that this will attract attention, so I have to remain standing. Then, whispering, we make an act of adoration together before the hidden God, the great Prisoner and Sufferer in the Holy Sacrament. Then he blesses me with the Blessed Sacrament in the simple eyeglass case. "Now off to bed, quickly," he tells me. In the morning when I get up, I ask him if he has slept well that night. He answers that after two o'clock he could not sleep anymore, but had kept the rest of the night vigil in adoration with Our Lord.

More than once, somewhere in the fields or secretly in a dormitory or in the attic of a workshop, Holy Mass is celebrated. Our Polish confreres from Krakow have done so several times as well. A couple of insiders keep vigilance in a wide circle. At first, it looks as if all are intensely involved with the work they are doing. But one of them bows over the bread and wine devoutly, speaking the words of consecration. The priest is not wearing a chasuble; no candles are burning during this holy moment. In a glance, nothing about what is happening can raise any suspicion. In great earnest and devotion, these priests in rags celebrate the Secret Prayers. As a chalice they use a glass or a cup, but the Lord descends among them in the substance of the bread and wine in the same way as in the most beautiful church or immense cathedral. Sometimes no host is available; instead the clerics bake a few grains of corn, which are consecrated by the priest.

One day, our Polish confrere, Father Albertus Urbanski, offers me Holy Communion like this. I ask Titus first if this is permitted. He answers that it is certainly all right to receive this form of Holy Communion, considering the abnormal circumstances we find ourselves in. I must say that it was an exception, and from the moment we received help from outside the camp, the Polish priests did not have to celebrate in such a manner any longer either.

In what way did we get help from outside the camp? In the little town of Dachau, lived a family with two children, a boy and a girl. This family was well known to the pastor of the St. Jacob's Parish, Father Pfanzelt. This priest chose one of the children to undertake a loving but dangerous act. The little girl regularly received a number of consecrated hosts to bring to the imprisoned priests who work outside the camp. The parish priest found out that the captured priests work at the Plantation and sends the child out to buy flowers. The Plantation happens to have a large nursery of gladioli that are to be processed into vitamin tablets later on, and many priests work there. Outside the camp fence, the child rides her bike in the direction of the gladioli fields. The guard, who stops her, believes her story and gives her permission to go ahead, which is a rare event in itself. She approaches the hothouses where the priests work. They are surprised to see a child. A little shy at first, she begins to talk with them and tells them she has seen a beautiful sacramental procession. It is the day of *Corpus Christi*. The clerics listen attentively and one of them sees how the child drops a small tin in the sand. Softly she whispers to one of the priests, "Our dear Lord is in there!" Then she walks off. She gets her flowers and happily cycles away. The priest who is nearest bends over and picks up the tin that holds the Holy Sacrament. So, totally unexpected, *Corpus Christi* becomes a real festive day for these priests, now that they are able to receive communion in this way.

After this day the girl returns many times, always pretending to come to buy flowers. All the guards get to know her so well that she can cycle through untroubled. Later, she also delivers unconsecrated hosts and wine so that priests, who are not allowed in Block 26, are able to celebrate the Holy Mass from time to time but always in secret. The priests in the camp soon give her the name of the "little angel!"

Also in other areas the clergy, regardless of their nationality, have found ways to practice their priestly ministry. As I said before, everything happens with great precaution taken and in secrecy. This is also true for the hearing of confession. Let alone to protect the dignity of this sacrament, we have to act very cautiously. Nevertheless, many confessions are heard. We know this also from other prisoners who have been able to confess. Apart from Holy Communion, it is almost the only sacrament that can be given inside the camp. You can see men walk in the company of a priest, and often it is not a private conversation but a spiritual dialogue, followed by a heartfelt confession. God alone knows how much good the priests did among the prisoners in this very aspect. Everything is done as inconspicuously as possible, most of the time in the street while hundreds walk past. Nothing in the appearance of the priest distinguishes him from the other prisoners. Sometimes you can tell by the serious look on their faces that a confession is being heard. Yet even that does not attract any attention, because there are plenty of other reasons to look serious. Only the attentive eye can sometimes see a slight movement of the hand by one of them, as he whispers the words *Ego te absolvo*, and thereby returns or increases the other's friendship with God.

Titus too exercised his priestly power among his fellow prisoners in this way during the short time that he stayed with us. He was always out to help others, especially on the spiritual level. Through his warm, open heartedness, he knows how to put someone's heart at ease in hard times, when one had nothing to look forward to. At such times, a favorite saying of his is "Dear friend, Dachau, with all its difficulties and dangers, is like a dark tunnel that we have to go through. We have to persevere and keep up our courage. At the end, the Light is radiating that will give us freedom." By that Light he means the Eternal Light that we have to aim for and that we have to keep before our eyes during all the difficulties of life. At these times, he always reminds us of the good Father who is in Heaven. His "Do your best and God will do the rest!" becomes almost proverbial.

Titus is failing visibly. The heavy labor, the daily fatigue, and the long marches wear away his strength at an ever-increasing pace. Just like all the others, he suffers terribly from hunger, and this prevents any healing of wounds that keep on deteriorating. Good advice in this matter is hard to come by. Among ourselves we discuss what needs to be done in order to improve his situation. Perhaps some people really want admission to the *Revier*, the camp hospital, if only for the bed rest that can help, more or less, to regain one's strength. On the other hand, the thought of taking him there is oppressive for us. We have our reasons. Patients are treated by fully unskilled people, people who became a nurse only because it is considered to be a "good job," a "better *Kommando*." There one gets a proper meal because the sick get extra food, although not in abundance and still quite bad and there is always the possibility of "organizing" something with the sick. Nursing is better than slavery anyway. You see, it is not especially inviting for us to be handed over to nurses who have neither knowledge nor love for their work and who are in no way held responsible if the sick die from their treatment. You always run the risk of being put on an "Invalid" transport which almost certainly means that death is near. Then there is always the fear of being used as a guinea pig by the professors and SS doctors in their studies of malaria or in their experimental application of cold-water, air-pressure or phlegmones. After all, the sick prisoners and especially the sick clergy are the best guinea pigs that anyone can possibly want. They are even cheaper than a rabbit and it means no loss for the Nazi system if they happen to die in the process. Personally I was used as a malaria guinea pig, so I know really well what it means to fall in the hands of these men. These are the reasons why you prefer to stay away from the *Revier* as long as you can.

One day around noon, at the end of my wits, I go to the *Revier* to have my own phlegmone wounds bound. In the infirmary, I happen to meet George, the head of the department, in person. I know how to get to him and I ask if there is any possibility of getting Father Titus Brandsma admitted to the camp hospital. "Titus? Who is Titus?" he asks. I tell him and describe his condition and he tells me to return the next day with Titus. I return to the block with this message and tell it to the Dutchmen. Everyone agrees that he needs to be admitted. The rest will do him good.

When we let Titus know what we think is best, he

says, "If that is what all of you think, then, in God's name, let's go!" The next day everyone wishes him a speedy recovery. Around 11:30 I take him to the *Revier*, supporting him on my arm. The head of the department is already there and, when he sees both of us coming in, he says "There he comes with his doctor!" In a way, that really surprises us, since very little friendliness can be expected here. Immediately he begins talking and carries on a conversation with Titus. He even cleans the wounds personally. For about a quarter of an hour, they have an animated conversation. Then the head nurse tells me "You can go back to your block. I will see to it that he gets a bed here." I say goodbye to Titus. He thanks me for all the help and sends his greetings to all the others on our block. "It is only for a few days," he says. And then he adds, laughing, "By August we will all be back home anyway, little brother." That is what he always said. Those are the last words that I heard from his mouth. We never saw him again.

LIGHT IN THE DEEPEST DARKNESS

In those days, there is no contact between our block and the *Revier* like there is later on, so we cannot go there for a short visit. However, a German priest, Gerhard Maashänser from Paderborn, is in touch with one of the nurses from time to time. This nurse is a really good Catholic and, compared to the rest of the nurses, an exception to the rule. His name is Fritz Kühr and he is Dr. Brüning's private secretary. Time and time again, he gets consecrated hosts from the above-mentioned priest and brings them to the patients who want to receive Holy Communion. So Titus still enjoys the real and unexpected pleasure of being allowed to receive Holy Communion. It is his last comfort here below, a last strength for the big journey that he will soon have to begin. Now he waits calmly for the ever closer end. Recovery is no longer to be expected, humanly speaking. Not only his exhausted body and festering wounds deprive him of his last strength, but so do the serious complaints that have been troubling him already for years— recurrent gastric bleeding and a urinary tract infection. He lies there, helpless, for a few days. It is almost the end of the dark tunnel in which he makes the last station of his Way to the Cross. Very soon he will reach his Calvary under the cross, giving a last glance towards Him for whom he has suffered so much.

The Polish Carmelite Hilarius Januszewski has been admitted to the same barracks and sees him several times at his sickbed. This is certainly a great comfort to Titus, as are warm words from the good Pallotine Father Josef Kentenich. It is almost certain that he has been

anointed during this last struggle. Soon after this, he los-
es consciousness and a weak rattling gives notice of his
approaching death. In the prison in Scheveningen, he
wrote a poem that since has become well-known everywhere. "*To enter here I will have none, I weary not when
I'm alone.*" Solitary and alone, he feels the end drawing
near. He dies in the same way that many die here—
slowly fading away without much notice taken. No
friends or confreres are with him. No one is allowed to
render assistance in his last moments. That is the last
sacrifice that he has to make here below.

It is Sunday, July 26, 1942. The nurse passes a message onto the Registration Office that number 30492
has died. His body is cremated the next day. Yet the
Light that he talked about so often during his stay in
Dachau appears to him at his death. He has reached
the end of the "dark tunnel" and is now taken up in
the eternal glory that he has so ardently desired. To become united with Christ by patiently suffering his
cross here on earth as far as Calvary has been his only
hope. He has fulfilled it. The last stanza of his poem –
a fervent longing to be with Jesus – is completely fulfilled in his death:

> *For Jesus you are at my side.*
> *Never so close did we abide.*
> *Stay with me Jesus, my delight,*
> *Your presence near makes all things right.*

The first notice of his death hits us like a thunder-
bolt out of the blue. Even though it was foreseen, it
comes unexpectedly. It is a Sunday afternoon. When I
see the head of the barracks, he calls me over and once
again the satanic in his person comes out. Sneering, he

holds out the official notice where the fact of Titus'
death is tersely reported. I read:

Anno Sjoerd Brandsma
Born: 23–02-1881 Prisoner No 30942

Block 28/3 died: July 26, 1942; 14.00 h.

+Departure by death
Concentration Camp Dachau 3K w.g.
(Revier, Registration Office)

With a sardonic sneer he grabs the paper out of my
hands and pours his heart out with a torrent of ob-
scenities and insults against priests and the priestly
state. However, they are all empty words to me. We
know what we have lost in the deceased. Or rather,
what we have won, for from the moment that he can
no longer be reckoned among the living, everyone
holds him fixed in his memory as a martyr. In truth, I
must say (I don't know if it is allowed really), I have
never prayed for him or his soul. I have prayed to him!
For us, there is no doubt that through his death the
gate of Heaven opened for Father Titus.

*The day after Titus died by a lethal injection in the
wrist, Father Henny Zwaans dies in the same sick barracks of exhaustion and dysentery after an imprisonment
of one year. Having to miss both his friends affects
Raphael deeply. He finds it extremely hard to hold out,
both physically and mentally. "How often I wished to be
in their place, to be released and able to rest and called by
the good God," he sighs several times. He continues on,*

concluding that apparently in God's eyes he is not yet ready for such an election.

In the hard days that follow, I often pray to Titus, who has known the dangers and difficulties of the camp from personal experience, to tell me if I will ever come out of this hell alive or if I shall have to die from starvation and deprivation as well. Each time I am brooding like this, it is as if Titus is standing right in front of me, saying "My little brother, however long it will take, believe me, you will get back home!" Though it takes weeks, months, even years, his words come true. The thought of coming out alive keeps you going, although you are never sure of your life. Here the devil is in charge but Heaven is with us!

The entire life in a concentration camp, with all its suffering and injustice, can be looked at in two ways. One can see it exclusively from the human point of view, but it can also be seen from a Christian stance. Only seeing the human side would really drive you mad out of pure revenge or maybe make you numb with grief. From a much higher point of view, you can do nothing but admit that the good Lord is indeed very kind to us to use us to bear all these things to His great honour and glory and in salvation of all souls. "For the Lord disciplines the one whom he loves." Is that not to be found in one of the Gospels?

Thank God, I am released from my first heavy *Kommando* since I am admitted to the *Revier* because of phlegmone wounds on my feet. After I am dismissed, still uncured, I do not return to my previous job. When the usual three days *Schonung* are over, I am assigned to a new labor *Kommando*, the so-called Ski *Kommando*. Thousands of skis meant for the eastern front have to be painted white. Anyway, the work is much more peaceful. Four of us sit and paint from a big jar— two German clerics, a priest, and a deacon from Kleve, a "Magnophat" as he keeps calling himself, and myself. It certainly is not bad work, but unfortunately it will not last long.

Hunger is torturing us more and more each day. Both of these German clerics are in Block 26; there life in general is better than on Block 28, where the hated Polish people as well as the Dutch are staying. They find it hard to see me languishing each day. Notwithstanding the risks, they help me wherever they can. From time to time, food is for sale in the canteen, be it carrots, lettuce or endive. Most of the time, some kind of collective punishment is going on in our block and it always concerns buying food in the canteen. It is a miracle if anything ever ends up in Block 28. My German friends, however, see to my needs. When I arrive at work in the afternoon, the good Reinhold Friedrichs has some carrots or turnips under his jacket or in the pocket of his pants. He watches how I eat everything in gratitude and with joy.

Hunger has certainly been the hardest ordeal in Dachau, but it was also the most informative time. Many of us in the priests' barracks are no more than living skeletons, emaciated frames. Then we get swollen all of a sudden, but this time it is the water, a harbinger of death, that accumulates in our bodies. In many cases, it is possible to foresee the number of days somebody has left to live. Dying comes about as a systematic process almost. Such people show typical symptoms. Some get very irritable and out of sorts for no reason at all. Others pine away slowly, without noticing themselves.

This becomes especially obvious in the evening as bread is distributed. What else can you expect? Who is able to divide the scanty portion of bread in an honest and just way? A whole loaf of bread has to be shared between four or five and that is a hell of a job. With a stingy look in their eyes, they gather around and watch how the divider puts the knife into the bread. It takes twenty minutes to reach the point that four pieces of bread are actually on the table, and then lots need to be drawn, although each piece looks to be the same weight— the dividing involves the use of a ruler with a centimeter scale. Each of the four pieces gets a piece of paper on top with the name of one of the persons concerned. After unfolding the paper, the name of the person who is going to receive that particular piece is read out. Sometimes a "neutral" person comes to watch, and in this way the owner of each piece of bread is chosen!

I have to say that hunger can make people do things that are unthinkable under normal circumstances. How often have I seen Russians, and other prisoners as well, risk their lives to snap up a carrot or a piece of cabbage. If an SS officer catches them in such a "crime," they run the risk of being shot on the spot.

There is only one thought in your mind and that is food: crusts of bread are a delicacy and carrots and beets too, even if they have been in the bin for quite a while. These are normal events. It also happens that in some of the transports that arrive after many days or sometimes weeks, and where prisoners had to survive with no food at all, corpses of fellow prisoners who died on the way are found with pieces of flesh cut off to serve as food. I know somebody who had worked for a long time in a *Kommando* that had to bring corpses to the crematorium. One day they had to carry garbage as well, and in the bins of the SS hospital they find the little corpse of a newborn baby. The sinister find is not really a shock to my friend, but what frightens him is when he finds out that it has been partly eaten. It is a devilish torture, hunger, one of the worst I have learned to know in Dachau.

However, not only hunger is a torment. There are plenty of other things that undermine the vital strength of the prisoners. There is the uncertainty, the pushing, always trying not to be conspicuous. It eats away at the nerves. It paralyses the muscles and makes you end up in a state of dull resignation. I can still see the hundreds of new arrivals. Sometimes they are more than a thousand standing at the assembly ground— like a slave market in the old days, but much worse. These modern slaves are naked, stripped of everything that rightfully belongs to them. Here one can see clearly how tiny a human being is and, in the way they deal with him, worse than slaughter cattle. Scenes like these are daily routine. They do not affect you that much anymore. You harden. In the depths of your heart you feel sorry for these poor souls when you think about them. Where they will end up, no one knows. Probably it will be another transport again, meaning death for many, if not all of them.

For the hundredth time Raphael is admitted to the camp hospital because of dysentery and big open wounds on his feet. Due to shortage of room, he and two priests are put on a closed ward with barred windows. They find themselves among nine severely mentally ill patients. It is a great relief to them when they are finally discharged and, after three days of Schonung, are allowed to return to their own barracks. Together, they have prayed quite a lot to be assigned to an endurable Kommando. *One of them ends up in the stocking darning workshop, a dark cellar where many priests, most of them old and handicapped, pass their days in peace. The other gets a job in the cleaning service. You can see him in the streets, strolling inconspicuously, with a small bucket in his hand into which he throws the "lost items."*

I get a good *Kommando* as well, namely the much desired *Mohrrube Kommando*. Daily, wagonloads of boiled carrots are cleaned here and afterwards transported to a sausage factory in Dachau. This job is one of the most favored, because during work one can eat some now and then, as long as that does not go too far. To insure against that, a specially assigned prisoner goes between the rows to prevent us from hiding carrots to take outside, something which is strictly forbidden, of course.

We are seated around a box and scrape our carrots, while, all the time, hungry people are peering in at the windows, hoping to get a carrot. I can also see my Dutch confreres standing at the windows and their looks equally show their thoughts: hunger, hunger, and more hunger. Whenever the guard is away for a few moments, carrots are flying through the windows to the outside, which almost causes a fight. This too comes to an end, and once again, I belong to the *Uneingeteilten*, the ones without a *Kommando*, which is very unpleasant, because they can come and get you for no matter what. This turned out exactly to be the way things would go for me this time.

FORLORN AND FORSAKEN

Saturday afternoon, November 19, 1942, I am walking down the block street where a lot of us are busy cleaning all kinds of furniture. Everything is out on the street again, tables, stools, lockers, etc— the usual cleaning that actually happens every Saturday. Suddenly the head of the block comes out of the door and calls me, saying, "Tuus, come here." He always calls me that because, as a German, he has difficulties pronouncing my real name. I walk towards him; at his side I see someone from the Labor Office. He has a piece of paper in his hand with some names on it and he says to the man next to him "Well, now you have the five you asked for." Apparently he is satisfied, and together we walk in the direction of the Labor Office. Nobody really knows what is going on. Innocently, I think I will probably be assigned to a new *Kommando* on Monday.

We arrive at the office where the five of us have to wait outside for an hour or more in lines of five since there are a lot more people. Patiently, we wait until someone comes and gives us a sign to follow him. We cross the street in the direction of the *Revier*. When we ask the clerk what this is all about, there is no answer. Once again, we have to wait in the hall for over an hour. We ask the nurses if they could tell us why we have to stand here for so long, but every time the answer is "You have lost of time, have you not? Why get so excited?" Yes indeed, time is what we have. Yet it all seems so strange to us. Finally one of the head nurses comes and asks the clerk "Are these the ones?" Yes, we are! In turn, he inquires whether we have been ill. The

elder in our group, a Polish priest, answers that he has
a hernia and is a gastric patient. He is sent off. The
next one is "all right." Now it is my turn, and although
it has been only a few weeks since I left the *Revier* with
serious dysentery, I decide to answer that I am in good
health. By doing so, I get the qualification "fit."

Now they take us to *Aufnahme*, the office where all
incoming patients are registered. We walk across a
small court where, as a rule, everyone has to hand over
his shoes. The *Kalfactor* on duty gives us a number in
return that serves to get one's shoes back later on. This
time we do not get anything back because we are registered as "patients." Next, we go to the ward in Block 1,
Stube 3. Again, our names are written down and then
they put us in bed. This makes us into patients, and although we try more than once to get away from here,
all our efforts are in vain.

So we stay in bed for some days without anything
happening to us. On Thursday, November 24, the feast
day of St. John of the Cross,[1] at nine o'clock in the
morning they call for us, and a nurse takes us to a department where an SS doctor is waiting for us. The
nurse exchanges a few words with the doctor, while we
are standing in the doorway wrapped up in only a blanket. The first one is called in, and the doctor takes some
blood out of his one arm to inject some other blood into the other. The rest of us get the same treatment in
turn. The SS doctor does his job without saying a word,
and so I get my injection too.

Then we go back and lie in our beds, but nothing
happens for the time being. However, now we know:

---

[1] John of the Cross's feast day is now celebrated on December 14.
In those days, it was celebrated on November 24.

we have become malaria guinea pigs. After a week, still nothing has changed, everything stays the way it is. My Polish fellow-sufferers have not come down with a fever either. That is what we are waiting for now. Every morning at ten, three SS doctors go past our beds to throw a passing glance at the fever charts that hang on the foot of all the beds. As soon as they spot a sudden increase in temperature, they ask the head nurse, never the patient himself, how this man is doing. We, as patients, have strict orders never to speak to the doctor or ask him anything. In cases where there is really something special going on with one of the patients, the doctor orders the nurse to do this or that or to administer these and those tablets.

The five of us, so-called *Malaristen*, lie among a large number of phlegmone patients, all subjects of medical experiments as well. During the weeks that we lie here, we get three tablets every quarter of an hour each day: every fifteen minutes, from six in the morning until midnight, three pills with a sick taste of cloying sweetness comes to 216 tablets per day! Add to this that I was already given such pills, with no result of course, a few months ago when I suffered from dysentery … and now we have exactly the same tablets against malaria!

After lying down for about a fortnight without any noticeable symptoms of illness, all of the sudden, a fever comes on at one o'clock. It returns every other day with such a force that the bed is shaking all over and it is almost impossible to count my pulse; the rate is over 150 per minute. Each time, my neighbors, the Polish priests, lend me a couple of blankets, as I bathe in cold sweat. Such a situation lasts exactly one hour and a half, always followed by a terrible headache accompanied by a thirst that drives you mad. When the doctors come the next day, they encircle the highest temperature on the chart in green with a happy smile. The first time, it is only 40.7 C. The next day I am free from fever, but the day after that, it returns with the same force at the same time.

One is not able to relax for one moment during the day. There is never a chance of falling asleep in peace, because the nurse comes again, using a pair of tweezers to place three tablets very precisely into my mouth while not getting close to me. After a while, this is so revolting that you cannot get anything past your gorge. You are sick of everything. My neighbor from Poland gets different tablets for the same malaria; it is a test and part of the experiment. His are not that sweet, he tells me, and so he proposes that I give some of mine to him from time to time, just to get a different taste in his mouth. Well, I have no objection at all, and as soon as the nurse comes to throw the tablets at me from a distance, I turn my head a little so that he misses and the little pills roll down the blanket. I pretend to put them in my mouth, but in fact I keep them in my hand, and when the nurse has disappeared, I give them to Father Stacek, who is really feasting.

The high fevers return regularly, and I suffer a burning headache which nothing relieves. In the end I decide to ask the SS doctors for some advice on their next visit, although this is strictly forbidden. The doctors pause at the foot end of the bed and whisper something to one another. They want to go on but now I dare to ask one of them for a medicine for my headache. Politely, in the same manner as I ask him, he tells the head nurse, "Give this man cold compresses." Over the shoulder of the doctor, I can just see the furious looks of the ward nurse, but as soon as he gets the order to give me cold compresses, his face gives an artificially friendly, "Certainly doctor, I will see to it." Then the doctors continue their round. I never saw one cold compress, but received something else instead. It is not difficult to guess what.

Again the fever returns at the usual time; again my temperature rises up to 40.6 C and more. The pulse beats mercilessly, and the bed is shaking right and left. During the malaria experiment, we have to fast in the morning till a blood sample is taken. This happens every morning. Probably it is intended for research and also for infecting other healthy people. Often the nurse takes a long time before collecting blood, so it often happens that it is already eight o'clock before we can bring the first drops of coffee to our dry lips. This is immediately followed by the scrubbing and polishing of the floor so that everything is spic and span by ten o'clock when the medical staff comes and visits us. The rest of the morning there is complete silence, as long as the nurses do not break it themselves. It is hardly possible to sleep. Each hour the "pill man" appears at your bed four times, without saying a word, to throw three calcium pills into your mouth. At night you are not left in peace either. A night watchman comes to take your temperature and pulse. No need to say in what way such a treatment affects your condition in the long run. It is easy to see how tiring and nerve-racking this is. After a couple of weeks, a few drops of Digitalis are prescribed for some time to strengthen the heart that has gone through quite a bit of work by now. We, starving men, welcome the green medicine with a sweet taste as if it were a delicious liquor. We regret that is only poured out in such a small quantity!

The only effective medicine, quinine, is not distributed, of course, since the purpose is the discovery of a new, German medicine. In his opinion, the malaria professor, we call him the malaria killer, has invented just such a medicine and he wants to experiment on us now. On a regular basis patients get his "syrup" as we call it. Indeed, after some time a few Polish clergy are cured remarkably quick. The professor is very pleased now that he has finally discovered a cure after such a long time. In Berlin he gets a patent for the new medicine and it is shipped to the various fronts where soldiers are suffering from malaria. After a couple of months, he receives the appalling news that all the soldiers that have swallowed his medicine have died. How is it possible that soldiers are dying, whereas the experimental prisoners are all cured? This needs a thorough investigation, and unfortunately the answer is found! What was the problem? In their letters to relatives, the Polish priests have mentioned in covert terms that they suffer from malaria. The relatives have hidden plenty of quinine in the first food parcels that are allowed them. In this way these *Malaristen* have the only effective medicine for malaria at their disposal. The malaria killer Schillings was convinced however, that the positive result was due to his own "syrup" and he was already dreaming of achieving fame in medical circles. When he finds out after close investigation how he has been mislead, his fury knows no bounds.

Weak and sick, I feel the end approaching slow but sure, and I really prepare myself for death. I would love to receive the final sacraments if possible. Although I am surrounded by at least fourteen priests, nobody is able to help me. Most of them are tied to their beds because of serious wounds and have to watch how some of their confreres go to Heaven from time to time. If anyone dares to pay even a short visit to a dying or dangerously ill patient, a guard turns up immediately to disperse the two with a push and a curse, because it is about time all this "confessing" is over with! How much you longed for a priest and a good word.

I do not care if I live or if I die now, I am prepared for anything. It would mean redemption, if the good Lord would come and take me during these dire times. Yet I want to be cured. Energy and the young life are really struggling indeed. I wait patiently, entirely surrendered to God's will, praying as far as praying is possible, because I often lack the strength. Good intentions, however, even turn the smallest word into a God-pleasing prayer, so through all the pain, I can only hope to live and do something good.

Slowly, very slowly I am making progress. A few times I manage to eat a bit of porridge and a couple of times an extra jacket potato. When the medical doctors have had enough, they order the nurse to finish me off. The administering of a special injection saves me from having more fever attacks.

With Christmas coming closer, I still find myself in the malaria ward of the *Revier*. Twice I have celebrated Christmas in a German prison, and I was going to spend another three in the camp. Despite the heartlessness of the nurses, there is something of an atmosphere of peace on Christmas Eve as well as on Christmas Day. Of course, my thoughts wander to family and homeland, brothers and sisters and my Carmelite confreres: what would their Christmas be like? I am having a really hard time. A terrible forlornness weighs on me and reminds me more than ever of the utter forsakenness of the Savior.

I lie among Polish priests; that is why I have only heard the singing of Polish Christmas Carols. How very beautiful the "Silent Night, Holy Night" sounds and how touching are the Polish carols. Although we cannot understand one word, their meaning is quite clear to us, because they all talk about the coming to earth of the Redeemer.

There is another Dutchman in the *Revier*, a Franciscan priest. He suffers from terrible phlegmones on his feet, but never does a complaint passes his lips. He endures even the most painful treatments by the doctors without uttering a sound. This gentleman is my companion in these days and we talk to each other a lot. He knows how to cheer you up and give you fresh courage. I thank God for putting him on my path. Sitting at the edge of my straw mattress, I listen to the gentle Polish Christmas Carols. Their tender melodies are gratifying to my heart and soul, so that we almost forget about the miserable concentration camp. Warm tears that we are not ashamed of at all, run down our hollow cheeks. We understand that as much as joy had been present in the stable, the same could happen in a camp as long as Christ is among us. Christ lives in our hearts, because a good friend of mine has brought us Holy Communion despite the great dangers that come with it. I will never forget those days!

Raphael is transferred to another sick barracks and manages to stay in the Revier *a bit longer to gain strength, but this time as a ward attendant. Among the sick are many priests. Whenever he can, Raphael sees to it that a priest can secretly make the sign of the cross on the forehead of someone dying. He helps take temperatures, distributes food, and assists during the twice weekly bandage hour. He is a quick learner and soon knows which oint-ment is to be put on which wound. There is not much to say about the medical training of the nurses. Infections on hands and feet are "treated" by instant amputation of the limb in question under the motto "what is not there any-more, cannot cause trouble any longer."*

The cruelty of experiments and treatments is beyond words. Especially in 1942 an admission to the Revier *means an almost certain death: ten to twenty die in one day, with exceptional days of over a hundred. One day the flag is out on the roof of the camp hospital. What is the matter? Is it to welcome a high-ranked visitor? No. It is not. That very day, not one patient has died!*

At the end of the year, there is a rumor going around that all foreign clerics, except for the ones from Poland, will be transferred to Block 26 where the German clergy live.

ROOM FOR THE MYSTERIOUS

Fortunately, the rumor is not only that, and after my dismissal from the *Revier*, I end up in Block 26, the barracks of the German priests. This means quite a change in the way we have to live in Dachau. Our situation improves drastically, because we are allowed to use the chapel now: every day we can attend Mass and receive Communion. To think that one has to end up in Dachau first to appreciate all this! Apart from that, being in Block 26 has the great advantage of less frequent beatings.

In these days, our first parcels from the Netherlands arrive, lifesavers for all of us. Without those parcels, nobody would have left the camp alive. One night, I receive a parcel from home with some warm underwear in it. It is a blessing now that it is so cold. Since we only wear a thin jacket and trousers, I immediately pull on my warm underwear. Apparently this is considered too much, because I have to hand over trousers and jacket, so all I am left with is this thick woollen underwear. However, I do look like a gentleman in them and I am much better dressed than most of the rest.

Meanwhile I work as a night nurse in the *Revier*, after having stayed there as a dysentery patient for some weeks. To prevent my friends who work with me in the night from becoming jealous, we settle on the following agreement. To protect us from the cold as much as possible, we will all be wearing my underwear in turn. As soon as my two hour shift is over, I yield the pants to the one who is in the next shift. This goes on for quite a while. You have to help each other whenever you can. Yet one has to be very careful, because the Communists are quick in drawing their own different conclusions. All day long you can hear their monologues on *Kameradschaft*, helping and supporting each other. Those who talk the most about these kinds of virtues, our *Stubenälteste* and *Blockälteste*, are by no means practitioners themselves; such is life and most certainly life inside a concentration camp. Being a night nurse is not an easy job at all: every night there are 30 to 40 sick to attend to, there is a shortage of free hands, and it is not always possible to be in the right spot at the right time. What makes it no easier is the fact that I am still recovering myself.

But troubles and fatigue do not count for much because I am lucky to receive Communion from a German priest every evening. He brings it to me in secret in a little piece of paper. I also have Holy Oil in a small ointment jar given to me by another priest, and each time a priest – most of my patients here are clerics – or somebody else is dying, I call for a priest in secret, who, in passing, traces a small cross on the forehead of the sick with the Holy Oil. We have to exercise the greatest care; if anyone should see this, the consequences would be immense.

Did I tell you about the things that are for sale in the camp? At ridiculously high prices, you can buy some sort of liquid product every now and then, for instance, beer. This is not the usual beer, but water with carbonic acid, funny tasting and it spoils quickly. We had to pour out so many barrels at our block, because it was simply impossible to drink, but nevertheless we must still pay for it. For a long time we are treated with *Gemüsewurst*. The name says it all: not a real sausage with meat and lard, but a five inch wide sausage made of only turnips and carrots only, held together with a lot of gelatine. Still you are willing to pay for such a delicacy. Another time there were ten kits of small salted mussels, at least a couple of years old and stinking to high Heaven. Although considered unfit to be eaten "outside," they end up inside the camp, where the hungry are not so choosy.

Sometimes the canteen sells uncooked food as well: carrots, turnips, cabbage, lettuce, endive and large ornamental pumpkins with tasteless watery pulp. Yet everything that comes in is welcomed as a real delicacy. Picture yourself as hungry, nibbling on a crescent shaped piece of pumpkin that gives just the sensation of a full stomach without having any food value whatever.

In 1943, nothing is for sale in the canteen anymore but substitute beer and lemonade. Nevertheless it is hard not to jump at the offer, because we are not only plagued by hunger but our thirst is unbearable as well. Drinking water is strictly forbidden, since the water is dangerously polluted and, so they say, makes you sick with typhus and dysentery.

As for clothing, we have to take care of that ourselves. That is why buttons, hooks and eyes are much sought after, though it is not allowed to have anything else in one's pocket but a handkerchief and a piece of toilet paper at the most. The few times that we get clean laundry, it is guaranteed that the previous owner has cut off all the buttons and hooks to save them for his "new gear." When outer clothes are worn out, they can be changed on *Tausch Tag* in the *Kammer* for another "zebra" jacket or trousers. We have to take off the badges – triangle and number – and sew them on the new outfit.

However, the day comes that they have run out of "zebra" clothes altogether, and from then on we wear civilian clothing of Jews that were killed and other deceased. Among the clothes, there could be high quality suits and whoever is lucky to find one, looks like a real gentleman. Due to scarcity, the only ones to wear the "zebra" uniform are those who work outside the camp and potential "runaways." What did they do to make the civilian clothes look like prison clothes? Very simple, you just cut a cross in the back of the coat and "repair" it by stitching a new cross of a different material on top of it.

Socks are rare indeed; the holes are repaired with patches and more patches on top of the old ones, etc. Footwear is true martyrdom. In the first year, I walked in slippers with wooden soles, then on a kind of wooden shoes. Walking in slippers is extremely difficult, especially when you have to go through mud and rain. Snow also sticks easily in big lumps under the feet, so that you can hardly move. I sweated water and blood when we had to march with such footgear. Add to this that all of us are suffering from hunger oedema and our swollen feet tingle with pain. We sustain wounds that turn into terrible phlegmones, something I already wrote about before.

When the first genuine clogs arrive, it is a moment of mercy for us; at least we can easily walk in these. Officially, they are called *Holländer*. It is not very long, however, before this glory is over with: most non-Dutch prisoners are not used to wearing clogs and soon the order "*Holländer abgeben!*" is issued. That is real bad news because I am so lucky to have a pair that fits well. Yet I dare not take the risk sabotaging the order. In the afternoon, at the parade, before marching out to work, all clogs have to be turned in, but I see my chance to get through unnoticed. At the Plantage, the

SS officer sees me walk by in clogs and he calls me over. He inquires why I did not obey the order to hand in the clogs. I answer that being Dutch I am used to walking in clogs without injuries from the day I was born. Without waiting for his reaction, I started running as fast as I can. This seems to impress the SS man; he whistles and calls for me once more. I fear inside that a terrible punishment will be the consequence of my action, but he smiles and says, "For you, I will make an exception, because you are born in *Holländer!*" And so for a long time, I am the only person in the camp wearing clogs!

Not only clothing identifies us as prisoners but our haircuts also make us immediately recognizable as prisoners in the outside world. Our hair is cropped close each week and inspected by the head of the barracks. If it is not properly done, he might just redo it himself! The shaven heads above the hollow cheeks give us real gallows faces, until the moment that it occurs to our tin god leaders that human hair is a valuable and precious raw material to certain industries. So the order comes that our hair is to be grown long. A human being is inclined to become attached to little when he has nothing. I cannot say how glad this new order makes us, now that our hair is longer. It is as if our humanity is increasing a bit as well. It is not long that we are able to rejoice in being allowed to have hair undisturbed. After a couple of weeks, an order comes that a strip, the width of a pair of clippers, is to be cut through the middle of our heads. The bold strip is soon called by its popular name *Hitlerstraße* (Hitler Street). The rest of the hair has to keep on growing and handed in at certain times. This now makes us equal to the Angora rabbits that are bred by the thousands in the camp for their fur!

The beard is shaven once a week. Ten or more are scraped by the block's hairdresser at a raving speed, because that is all there is to it. Taking a piece of skin more or less does not count very much. Later on, I am allowed to use my own shaving set because I suffer from a persistent barber's rash due to frequent shaving with the same knife over and over without using a disinfectant. Fortunately, I meet a Polish doctor at the Plantage who gives me a recipe that I include in covert terms in a letter home, and the necessary ointment is sent to me after some time.

It is a good thing that my pseudonym was understood at home; every second Sunday of the month, when we are allowed to write a letter, I can let them know all kinds of things. Only Germans are allowed to write twice a month. Because I gave our monastery in Mainz as my permanent address, I can write two letters each month too! The first sheet goes to my Carmelite confreres in Mainz and the second is written to my parents. Father Prior translates it and sends it to the Netherlands. In this way, I keep in touch with two addresses.

It is absolutely forbidden to write anything about the camp and its inmates or any other fact. You always have to write "Everything is fine. Do not worry about me" even when you are not far from dying. In case I want to write a bit more and about things that would certainly not pass the censor, I do the following. I write, "A few days ago, I also received a letter from Anton van Riessen (that is my pseudonym that I once wrote as an address); I am sure you would like to know what he is writing about, so I will repeat it here." Then

I can right very honestly about everything that is bothering me, how I am in fact really doing and a lot more. Thank God, they understood at home, though it might have occasioned some brain racking now and then. Father Prior regularly sends letters back with information about a certain Anton van Riessen, and in this way even the smartest SS-censor is tricked, and much more news got abroad than the guards cared for.

Everyone is allowed to write letters except for the Russians and the NN-prisoners. They are the *Nacht und Nebel* cases who arrived in Dachau from Natzweiler, an extermination camp. The initials "NN" says it all— people that disappear, vanished in the dark of night and clouds. They are condemned to death without trial. They are under strict surveillance for fear of escaping. That is why they never work in *Kommandos* outside the camp nor receive any parcels.

The situation on the block is still precarious for us clergy. We are beaten and battered for nothing at all, as I have said already. One day the head of the barracks calls for me and, instantly, I take my glasses off as if by habit, for I am convinced that I will receive at least a couple of boxes on the ear, with or without reason. While I stand in front of him, he asks mockingly why I always laugh at him the moment he hits me. In astonishment, I look at him for a short time but this is already cause enough for him to box my ears a few times. After I am back up on my feet, he repeats his question. I try to avoid him by stepping back a few paces, answering him by denial. "What!" he screams, "you are not laughing at me?" and his attitude gets even more provocative. A bit calmer, he continues, "But you are my enemy, so vice versa it will be the same no doubt, since you get beaten every day." "My enemy? You?" I ask in return. "I never said you were my enemy." His next question is whether I ever pray for him. "You guys preach that one should pray for the enemy, do you not?" I look him straight in the face, and because I know he was born Catholic, I tell him I pray a Hail Mary for him each time he beats me up. He stares at me in astonishment and from that day on, he never hits me again, not even once!

After reading about the many atrocities that living in Dachau brings, maybe many of you start to think: "Why did they not try to escape?" You will hardly believe it, but in the first years when everything was very tough and cruel, attempts to escape were rare. Later, when discipline is not that hard any more, someone would be missing at roll call much more frequently. Escaping from this life of hell is a desperate venture, seldom or never done successfully. Whoever succeeds will be located usually within two days. Then the consequences are immense. First of all, the camp is marked off with an electrified barbed wire fence, two meters in height. Behind that is a moat, three meters in width. Then, all around the industrial buildings and SS barracks that surround the camp is a high brick wall, with armed guards at each gate or entrance, both day and night. Furthermore, machine gun barrels are sticking out the window frames on three sides of the several watchtowers that are standing at the barbed wire fence. A volley of firing, especially during the night, is directed at the slightest movement in the area of the fence. How many times I have seen the bodies of those who have walked into the fence out of despair, only to be electrocuted at once, lying on the ground.

However, let us suppose an escape has been successful. Where can you go in the terrible prison uniform that we wear all the time? The camp authorities know very well that such a "zebra" outfit is not worn anywhere outside the camp and that it makes escaping more difficult. Even without that uniform, a child would have identified us as prisoners. The marks are on our faces, all our actions would make every "free man" immediately suspicious.

Then the punishments that await the poor victim after an unsuccessful attempt to escape! As soon as somebody is missing, everybody in the camp has to assemble on the parade for many, many hours until the escaped prisoner is tracked down. Of course, nobody cares about the weather; in rain or snow, we have to stand and keep standing. It happened once that the whole camp stood for 36 hours. I do not have to tell you about the mood we were in and how we felt about that particular escaped person. The unlucky soul has to stand near the camp entrance for days, march through the camp barefoot, and receive the much-feared 25 lashes. These lashes, with a bullwhip, are the most frequent punishment, given for various infractions and always executed in public in the assembly ground. Worse than the "25" is the so-called *Baum*, suspending prisoners from a tall pole by their hands bound behind their backs. The limbs are pulled from their joints and this causes terrible pain. In the first years, the SS also set bloodhounds at the naked victims, which rip them apart. When they are let down after a full hour of hanging, they are no longer humans but wrecks, not capable of doing any work. They cannot even bring a spoon to their mouths and sit at the table slurping their soup from the bowl. To help such victims is strictly forbidden. In later years, this punishment is cancelled and all data about prisoners who underwent this punishment was removed from the documents in such a way as to destroy any incriminating evidence.

Another official sentence is the *Stehbunker*. It is a small kind of cupboard, a narrow cell with hardly enough room to stand up. It is not possible to lie down, sit or squat, just to stand. In such a small cell, the victim has to persevere for some days, even some weeks. There is no ventilation, except a little fresh air that comes through small gaps underneath and above the door. The only possibility to relieve the most urgent human need is an old tin. Meals consist of some jacket potatoes, or maybe less, in cases where the verdict was such.

In the final year in the camp, running away became easier, because older SS men who had been dismissed from the front replaced the young SS guards. They see the end getting close and are fed up with everything anyway. Escaping becomes a daily event, especially for Russians. Each day at least hundred or more are "on their way," as we call it. Some of us really crave freedom and, although I have had the chance to escape at least a hundred times, it never occurred to me to actually do it. When I worked at the Post Office in 1944, I was at the station in the town of Dachau at five in the morning. From there, escaping would have been easy, but the consequences for the others at the block would not have been very pleasant at all.

As mentioned before, the replacement of the SS is a big improvement. The younger officers leave for the front and elder SS and men of the Wehrmacht *take over their positions. They are quieter, not so fanatical; they know things are in a bad way. The Communist staff are turned out of their nice jobs too. Now socialists from Austria sway the*

sceptre over the barracks. The clergy are granted less heavy
jobs, often getting work in the administration.

I am part of the *Postkommando*, a much desired and
excellent *Kommando*, especially the out-of-camp *Kom-*
mando that is in charge of collecting the parcels from
the station and the main post office. Every morning at
five, the post car drives out of the camp to return
around nine o'clock, and that means the end of the
working day also. You are free for the rest of the day
and have time to read, to draw and even to cook. For a
while, we have a "cooking church!"

Now that the physical needs are decreasing, we really start to feel the spiritual hunger. Though we are
laughing again, the desire for freedom, to return to full
life is growing. We are homesick for our families, our
homeland, our monastic life and our former ways, and
this destroys our peace of mind. The humiliations and
arbitrary treatments are hurting us more.

The story Raphael wrote down in 1945, straight after his
return to the Netherlands, stops here. That is to say that the
rest of his writings are missing from the files. However, it be-
comes obvious in the last part of his report that we have ar-
rived at the final year in the camp. The SS who are still pres-
ent try to save their skin by acting favorably to the priests.
The clerics used to be called Saupfaffen; *from the time the*
first parcels arrive and the position of the SS diminishes,
everywhere you can hear "Your honor" and "Mister priest."
The Nazis have started to evacuate other camps and they
send their inmates on death marches or on transport by cat-
tle cars to other camps situated in the eastern part of Ger-
many. Dachau is flooded with transports from all quarters.
It is impossible to handle the enormous flow. The once so

*perfect admission system is not functioning anymore. Clerics,
among them Raphael, are mobilised, as we read in his German notes.*

During the years 1944-1945 so many newcomers arrive daily that the *Schreibstube* can no longer do the
job. It happens often that we clerics are called in to
help. Please do not think of this as a pleasant job at all
or that there are a lot of interesting things to see. I will
always remember the time that an immense sick transport arrived from Natzweiler near Strasbourg. This is
an annihilation camp. The name says it all. Sick people
arrive in Dachau totally exhausted, many a man is dying. These are put out on the sharp gravel, without
mercy, in endless rows. Can you imagine what it
means to see such a desperate crowd lying helpless on
the ground, and there is nothing you can do to help,
not even the slightest thing, to ease their pain? Many
died as a consequence of the transport and dead bodies
are everywhere. When it is extremely cold, such transports go into the bathhouse, but that is the only con-
cession. Then you can see SS officers walking through
the human crowd, pointing out who is doomed to die
and can be removed. Now and then they kick someone
on the ground with their iron shoed boots, saying to
the nurses with a grin on their face, "This one is dead
already, or nearly there!"

We have to fill in the full names and addresses and
other information on forms. And the things you see!
There goes another *Rollwagen*, pulled by some of our
fellow inmates and loaded with the poor wretches, thin
as rails, as good as dead, headed in the direction of a barracks. How miserable they look. A bit further on, you
see hundreds of people lying on the ground, no more

than emaciated frames. Those who are still alive are pulled out and loaded on a car. Completely naked in the bitter cold, they are brought into one of the barracks. How I would have loved to help. However, we have nothing to comfort them with or to provide any kind of service for the poor fellows. I carry them from the cold winter night into the barracks on my back, see that they get a blanket, if possible two, a bit of bread and a mug of hot coffee and promise to come back as soon as possible. We never stop bringing in newcomers, all thin to the bones, many of them at the point of death.

One night, a newly arrived transport had to stay outside in the freezing cold overnight, naked. Nobody survived that particular night. In a heap of frozen corpses, they lay on top of each other. The next morning the corpses are cut loose and brought to the crematorium. There they are piled up, since the ovens cannot handle the large number, and the pile of frozen corpses is growing.

How many times at night I see those piles of emaciated corpses loom before me like a bogey. Afterwards, you wonder how you were able to cope with all these things without becoming insane by the sight of such a sub-human pandemonium. This ever-growing heap of corpses is burned in my memory, engraved in my mind as if chiselled in granite. You could see body parts had been cut off some corpses, and it was obvious that fellow prisoners had come to use their dead comrades' bodies to prevent themselves from starving. These are neither fantasies nor sensationalism; it is the raw truth that I want to show, however horrible it is.

Later on, when I am promoted to *Bürogehilfen*, a kind of administrator, I get to see a totally different side. Fellow prisoners confiscate anything of value. In the years

41-42, all belongings were still taken by the administration and kept in bags. Now all kinds of things, watches, rings, and toiletries disappear into the pockets of "friends." Clothing is thrown on a heap, taken to the Disinfectant Department and distributed for general use. A big cross is stitched onto the jackets. In this way, everyone in Dachau has literally to bear his cross.

Each day something different happens. Every prisoner could well write a book about it, especially the clerics. In our *Stube* is an aged priest, 82 years old, from the vicinity of Vilnius in Lithuania. He was a prisoner in Siberia for five years under the regime of the Tsar. After six months in Dachau you hear him say, "I would much rather be in Siberia!" A German Franciscan, named Gassmann, who spent almost three years in Siberia, says the same thing.

Despite everything, there have been nice moments as well. The good moments in Dachau are all religious in character. You can see faithful Christians really live their faith here. From the moment I arrived in the camp and my habit and everything was taken away from me, my ties with the past were broken but I felt more and more guided by God. He is the One with whom I feel connected in all circumstances. His omnipresence, a truth that was once not much more than theory, is an intense experience here and takes shape in a way that often feels benevolent. His providence is the pillow where we lay our tormented souls at rest. You know God will lead you. No matter what may happen, it only happens according to His will. In the absence of human satisfaction, one achieves the complete surrender to God's providence, and thus to God. Lack of everything that is needed to live creates more room for the Mysterious.

I must confess that every now and then I look back to those difficult years with some feeling of nostalgia. Never have I felt closer to God. The electrified barbed wire could not prevent God from reaching us. Praying became an inner necessity, not as a rule or a prescription or out of annoyance, but it was simply the only thing to do. I have never prayed more often and more fervently than here. The more forbidden, the more the soul clings to prayer. A piece of rope with ten knots serves as a rosary; a hidden medallion is a real treasure. The more we have to bear and to endure, the more intense we are entwined with the supernatural. The greater the torture and maltreatment, the closer we feel attached to the Passion of Christ. Heaven is approaching us.

At the end of 1944, camp life is getting worse in a number of aspects. The flow of parcels from the Netherlands stops, due to acts of war; the spectre of hunger is coming back. Thanks to our German confreres, who let us share in their food parcels that do get through to the camp, we are saved from starvation. From the point of view of sanitary conditions life becomes true martyrdom, now that the population of the camp has increased up to 40,000 souls. The barracks are overcrowded and many perish in the filth and dirt. The communal bathing, often a hundred at a time, is abolished. A change of underwear or clothing is getting more rare. Changing gear once every four or six months— the consequences are not hard to guess. Soon the whole camp is overrun with vermin of all sorts, instigators of all kinds of illnesses like the killer typhus. All barracks are ordered *Lauskontrolle*, lice inspection. Everybody, naked above the waist, has to go past a couple of inspectors, who are busy chasing the "little animals." The Dutchmen who live on our block certainly have their reputation for being clean to lose! If something is detected, you have to go to the disinfecting. Here, you have to hand in all your clothes that are then treated with gas. Your entire body is smeared with some stinging stuff. This can take all afternoon. Often you do not return before the next day. It is hard to comprehend what this means. To stay warm, you make all kinds of movements or stand close to a friend to keep each other warm. Sleeping is out of the question and the next morning the nerve wracking rushing and slavery starts again. Worst of all, when you get back after such a treatment, the lice are not gone at all, or they return within no time, since you are in physical contact with others all the time.

The story of Raphael comes to a conclusion during the final months of his stay in Dachau, when he reaches the theme of liberation in his German diary. In the chronologically written account of that intense time, he resumes the style of the eyewitness, so that we can read a moving account of the liberation of the camp by the Americans.

Daily events and action in the war are becoming more interesting to us, for we feel our liberation is getting near, now that the allies come closer.

You might wonder how we keep ourselves informed of what is going on outside the camp. First of all, there are the daily newspapers that reach us in the camp. In these we read about the activities at the war front. At the end, we are able to listen to the English radio broadcasts. This is done in secret, of course, by some prisoners who work outside the camp. Their messages, so-called *parolen*, spread through the entire camp like a wildfire, causing a sensation and excitement among the inmates. Thus, we hear that the allies are pressing onward more and more. Also the continuing heavy bombing of Munich, Nürnberg, Augsburg, and Regensburg are some of the omens of the approaching end. But news about the war in the Netherlands makes me worry. Often my thoughts go to my dear parents. Am I to see them again, or shall fate take them away from me at the very last moment?

WHY EVER ALL THIS? WHY?

The American army has already reached the Rhine river. You will perhaps understand how tension is building up and coming to a climax. What are we up against? What will happen to us? Shall we be put on a transport? Everyone knows what that means. Some of us who survived such a transport told the most awful stories about it. At a certain moment, we no longer have newspapers, but pieces of news penetrate into the camp nevertheless. Daily, bombers fly across the camp and sirens of the air raid alarm are rife. There is a rumor going around. "If the warning alert sounds for five minutes at a stretch, then armored tanks are advancing."

On Thursday, April 26, an order is issued to evacuate the entire camp, and tension runs high. Around noon, everybody in the camp is assembled on the parade ground with blankets and all kinds of travel needs that could be of use in case of a retreat. The square is a scene of thousands and thousands of men, all in fearful anticipation of what is to come. Maybe you feel the same as I did at the time: to be carried off into the unknown, who knows, maybe even driven to death. There they are, the many thousands; a terrible fear is depicted on every countenance. Tension tightens their hollow cheeks around their prominent jaws. Could it be that we will eventually go to the wall at the very last moment, after having won over all the torments? Oh my God, the thought of it is unbearable. I have always dreaded this moment, trembling at the idea. All kinds of rumors go about, like a transport that is to go to Ty-

rol. That would be a march of a couple of days. I
would never be able to make it. Somewhere in the
Alps, I would collapse, a bullet or rifle-butt would put
an end to my life. Was I never to see my beloved homeland again? How often had I looked death straight in
the eyes, but I have never been as frightened as this
time.

We are on the assembly ground, waiting for further
orders. It takes hours and hours, and little by little, you
see more people disappearing into the barracks. Our
barracks is all together empty, even the old familiar
chapel. What a desperate place it is now. The empty,
open tabernacle reminds me of Good Friday. Will this
empty room, witness to so many joys and sorrows, never celebrate the *Te Deum* of our liberation in the end?

In Dachau, you can never know anything about the
future for certain and everything will work out much
different than many of us feared. Notwithstanding, all
Reich-Germans, Russians, Bulgars, Rumanians, Jews,
and gypsies have to stand apart; these groups are under
severe surveillance. Finally, a group of 8000 men receive a bread ration to last for four days. By the
evening they leave.

*A couple of weeks earlier, a small number of priests had
been released. One of them, Otto Pies, hears of this large
transport and fears the worst. On his bicycle, he goes after
it and overtakes it south of Munich. He notices several of
his brother priests among the overdriven and worn out
men. He throws some clothing towards them, which they
put on in a rush so that they can escape. Then he returns
with a van loaded with bread. The commander-in-charge
is gotten drunk on cognac and Pies tells him that, by order
of the Red Cross, all clerics with injured feet have to go*

with him in the van. He gets permission to do so. In this way, he saves 44 out of 89 confreres.

He returns a second time with his van, but does not succeed in getting through to the group. Many from this transport have escaped, but many more have died, staying behind alongside the road, exhausted and tired out, to be shot by the SS. Yet the march keeps going on, although the rows get thinner. After five days, they reach Bad-Tolz. In the meantime, American troops have already liberated the Dachau camp.

The past days find us in a continuous state of tumult. Every morning we stand on the assembly ground, waiting for the order to march out as well, but each time the order is withdrawn. Until that Saturday morning, on April 28, at nine o'clock, when wailing sirens are heard during five minutes. "Armored tanks advancing!" An unimaginable agitation takes hold of us. All transports sound the retreat. What awaits us now? Is it really true that American armored infantry have come to liberate us? Sure! The liberators are coming closer and closer. As it turns out though, the alarm is signalling that the entire SS staff is to gather to help put down a major insurrection that has broken out in Bavaria.

Within the camp tension is rising higher and higher as we can hardly wait the moment that will mean our rescue. On the morning of Sunday, April 29, the flag is hoisted at the entrance of the camp. The white flag of capitulation! The SS take to their heels! It is said that *Wehrmacht* men are coming to take over guarding and hand the camp over to the allies. Maintaining order within the camp would be our job then. Needed measures have already been taken, since we fear that Russians will ransack and commit mass murder. We have called forth a well organised, though unarmed, police force. Thank God, it never comes to a violent clash.

That particular Sunday, around twelve, our own head of the block (for a couple of months, block staff have come from our ranks) announces the flight of the SS and that the white flag of surrender is flying from the entrance gate. What a great joy! Our rescue is near. Jubilant and rejoicing, the noise is enough to awake "the seven sleepers."

How simple and naïve we were to give any credence to the statements of the SS. Are we still that "green," after being disappointed so many times? After the liberation, we find a message from Himmler in which he orders that nobody is to fall into the hands of the enemy alive. "Evacuate or liquidate," says the telex that Himmler sent to camp commander Weiss, when the latter inquires what to do now that the enemy is advancing. The original plan was to evacuate the entire camp but the approaching march of the American army stopped this. Just a small number of the 40,000 inmates are carried off; those are the 8,000 men I already mentioned before. It is Himmler's intention that the rest are to be liquidated. Later on, it turns out that the so-called *Wehrmacht* who were to take over the camp, are, in fact, a bunch of Viking-SS. They could be trusted to exterminate the camp!

We are not, in any way, aware of all these things yet. Had we known, I am afraid it would have lead to terrible actions with incalculable consequences: 32,000 people would have defended themselves to the death. Yet since we are unaware of all the perils that are threatening us, we put just too much trust in the SS. We are as happy as children. Any minute now our liberators will be here. It will not take much longer for sure. We hold our breath from the sheer tension, as the bombers skim the camp and air gunners fire at the anti-aircraft guns with machine gun salvos. What exactly is going on? Is it the Americans coming closer and closer or is it a handful of remaining SS fighting the allies?

All of a sudden, we hear that the SS criminal prisoners who are supposed to guard us have taken the watchtowers. They are former SS men who are serving their sentences of hard labor in separate barracks. In camp language, they are called "fallen angels." So, in the final moments of our camp life, we have fallen into the hands of this set of rogues!

Meanwhile, it is Sunday afternoon. The order "into the barracks, into the barracks" keeps on sounding. In the overcrowded *Stube* and halls we are praying aloud, still the best approved method to stay calm in times of trouble and danger. As we are pressed together inside the *Stube*, we hear machine guns crackling and rattling constantly, alternating with the roar of guns and heavy bombs bursting further in the distance. None of us realises fully that the battle for the camp is in full swing. We keep thinking all the time that it is all about military actions against other targets.

The fighting is getting nearer and nearer and we are able to distinguish separate shooting better and better. Sometimes it is so loud that you are frightened to death. What if the camp ends up in the middle of the line of fire, because then they will shoot the wooden barracks into matchwood. All kinds of sensible and inept thoughts flash through our minds. Fear is written on many a face. Nervousness is increasing, as the barracks is so overcrowded. Although it is strictly forbidden to go out in the block street, some of us are driven outside because of lack of space. Then, all of a sudden, a strident cry goes up, "Americans, Americans!"

Then I dare to go outside, and I notice the first Americans approaching in between the horse-stables and the SS-barracks. They come in small, separate groups. Crouching down low, they steal around the barracks, and now they are on the other side of the electric fence. First they do not see us at all; all they do is look around to see if there is danger somewhere, for at that very moment, machine guns start to crackle from the watchtowers. Suddenly, I spot an American sticking his *stengun* out of one of the windows of a watchtower. A moment later, a "fallen angel" leaves the watchtower, hands behind his neck, followed by a second one and a third one, a fourth, a fifth. They are all shot on the spot.

Meanwhile, people in the camp are beside themselves. They break out of the barracks in a massive wave that goes in the direction of the fence, towards the liberators! An enormous crowd presses itself against the fence. An unequalled triumph is breaking out. I can still see one of the American soldiers looking at us, giving us signs by moving his hands to stay calm. More and more people push forward to the fence. One wants to climb over it to get to the liberators; in the excitement he forgets about the deadly high voltage wires, touches them, and drops down. He has seen his liberators but has not lived to see his liberation. After some soldiers have entered the camp, they go up into the next watchtower. We can see them standing by the windows: all guns and ammunition are thrown out. They remove the bullets from the guns that were aimed down on the camp from three directions. The crowd is still moving like a churning mob. They scream and wave at the men above who will no longer give them gun volleys. How peaceful they stand there, laughing at us, and waving in a cheerful way. Films are made of the madding crowd. It is indescribable. Even a lot of sick have come out of the infirmary and are seen in the street, no matter what wounds or injuries they have. After the news of the arrival of the Americans reached them, they want to meet their liberators also. They walk around, with hardly any clothes on their exhausted bodies. On their frightened faces is written pain but also joy. Paper bandages, binding up their wounds, have come loose and wave like pennants behind them. Is it not a miracle that one nearly dies at the spot of sheer emotion?

Now we are heading to the *Jourhaus*, the strange name for the main entrance of the camp. Here, the SS are always present, to check everything and everyone that come in or goes out. Prisoners are only allowed to pass the gate bareheaded. Like a swelling wave during high tide, men move alongside the fence in the direction of the *Jourhaus*. Gradually more and more allies have joined us, the first armored vehicles are rolling inside the camp, and not much later one can see officers among them as well. The first thing to be done after entering the *Jourhaus* is to shut the electricity to the fence off, preventing more accidents from happening.

The joyful celebration on roll-call square is still going on. People fall into each other's arms, crying and dancing with sheer happiness. It is simply beyond comprehension that this day is finally here and we are free. It is Sunday afternoon, April 29, 1945, twenty-nine minutes past five. How could anyone who was there ever forget? Suddenly a soldier appears above the entrance gate, using gestures to appeal to the crowd for calm. It takes a long time before it gets quiet but people begin to understand that he wants to say something. Finally, the officer starts to speak, and his speech went something like this, "Comrades, although my German is not very good, I want to say a few words to you. You are free, Free, FREE. Free as we, Americans, are free." Storms of cheers rise up to heaven. "No longer do you need to fear any evil coming to you. However, you should not just thank us Americans for your liberation, but first of all God, Our Lord in heaven, for He has sent us in time to set you free. We will see that each one of you may return to his home country as soon as possible." After having spoken those delightful words, he raises his arms and, lifting up his eyes to Heaven, blesses all who are present. He turns out to be a Catholic chaplain in the American army! Nobody can keep his eyes dry any longer, and we feel that we have shaken off the hard, heavy yoke of the SS that has weighed on us for so many years.

A short while after these kind-hearted words, the iron gate opens and officers enter the camp. The celebrating crowd puts them up on their shoulders. First of all, they go to the *Revier*, the sick barracks, as it is justly feared that the worst misery is to be found there. They also pay a visit to the overcrowded "Invalid" barracks where bitter, gray, miserable circumstances prevail. Next, they go to the priest's barracks and the chapel. By eight o'clock, a festive *Te Deum* is celebrated to thank God dearly for his great kindness and mercy to set us free of slavery. That same evening, flags of the 24 different countries that are present in the camp wave on top of the barracks. Growing out of the roofs as it were, these flags spring up like mushrooms. It is indeed an impressive spectacle.

At the assembly ground, the scene of so many horrors – the coliseum of the 20th century as I once called it – a huge altar is set up. A giant wooden cross rises high against the sky. May 3, a High Mass is sung in the presence of all the American soldiers and prisoners. The next day, the 4th of May, a solemn *Requiem* is sung for all who have died or were killed in Dachau from its very beginning. It is a pity it rained that evening at eight. Nevertheless, the enormous assembly ground is black with people. Everyone commemorates their best comrades who gave their lives. Thousands upon thousands will never again return to their homeland. Numerous comrades have been cremated after they died, and many a road has been paved by the remains of their bones. We reminisce about them during this solemn hour of reflection, because each of us has lost one or more at least.

To give some statistics for the past months: in February, 1945, during the typhus epidemic, 3972 corpses have been burnt. In March, 3668 comrades died. Day and night black smoke came out of the chimney of the crematorium. The entire camp was overrun with the stench of corpses. Due to lack of coal, it is almost impossible to burn all the corpses, so they are piled up in huge heaps in front of the crematorium. The mortuaries too are packed to the roof with corpses. In the block street, each morning rows and rows of deceased who have departed this life and passed through the veil that night, lie on the ground. I have often gone past the rows to see if a friend or acquaintance is among the dead. In silence one prays the Our Father for those who have died, after which they are quickly loaded on a big cart for transport to the crematorium. The next morning, one can go alongside the sinister rows again, in the same way. As I said, lack of coal makes it impossible to burn the corpses; that is why four mass graves are created in which 3,500 comrades will be laid to rest.

After our liberation, between the 1st and 15th of May, another 1,433 of our comrades unfortunately die. How hard it must have been for them to have to die in Dachau, after being set free. Farmers, from the area around Dachau, are forced by the Americans to see that the deceased get a burial worthy of a human being. Every dead person is to have a grave of his own. No more mass graves are allowed. That must have been very difficult for them, because many corpses are already in an advanced state of decomposition. Many found their final resting place in Dachau's woodland graveyard, where 939 wooden crosses are still to be found.

Now that we are free at last, it is as if we finally make a new start with life. All of the sick from the *Revier* are placed under the care of the Americans. A large number of doctors arrive to treat the patients. The American army provides two field hospitals since there is a big shortage of beds. Even several French nuns come to nurse the sick. All the time, you see Red Cross cars driving them in and out of the camp. They are cared for until they have recovered enough that they are able to return to their own countries. Now the Catholic clerics get permission to minister in the infirmary too, something that was forbidden in the beginning. Thus they can give spiritual help to the sick and dying, and help many to prepare for their last journey.

An order is issued to plan for a thorough disinfecting of the camp, which is actually carried out since the entire camp is overrun with vermin, causing diseases like typhus. All inmates are treated with DDT powder several times, which leads to great results within a short period of time. More and more American soldiers come to the camp to visit all the barracks. There is a lively press, the entire camp is put on film and gramophone recordings are made of individual prisoners' eyewitness accounts.

After liberation, the food supply gets much better as well. Each morning starts with a nice soup and ham and cheese on bread, an unknown luxury before. The Americans meet our wishes in all possible ways and they give us plenty of attention. Yet deep inside us, the desire to go home is like a burning flame. We want to go home, home, home. Many can no longer wait for the day of their final release and they leave without official permission, which means without identity papers and on their own responsibility. Gradually, groups from various nationalities are put in quarantine before they are given permission to return to their homes.

During these days, the newly created camp police arrest several men whose behavior toward others could not pass muster. They are turned over to the Americans and given a summary conviction— in some cases, the death penalty is carried out. Former members of the SS, gradually tracked down in the camp, are taken to court and later convicted. Most of them die by hanging.

Very soon, they grant us more space to move around in, although we still have to remain within certain boundaries. However, we can walk as long and as much as we like in the beautiful woods that surround the camp and in the *wildpark*, a park with a swimming pool constructed by prisoners. The whole area once served as a recreation and amusement park, but to us prisoners it is unknown territory. Now we can walk around freely wherever we want and that means a great deal to us, who were allowed only one route for so many years. It is hard to grasp in the beginning, and often you walk around carefully and cautiously, as if you are still afraid of going too far.

One day, something very nice happens to me. One beautiful afternoon in spring, like every day after my liberation I went into the woods to enjoy the fresh spring air like never before. Without being aware of it, I get to the boundary of our vast camp. All of the sudden, I find myself opposite a grinning black man, with weapon in hand. "Stop! Where to?" he calls. Frightened to death, I can only stammer that I am just strolling. Immediately, another four black men surround me, and they lead me to a tent that they have erected behind some bushes. It turns out to be a merry crowd and immediately they bring in an accordion, and everybody sits down on the field beds. As for me, I do not feel like laughing at all, because I have no idea what they are up to. However, one of them, seated on his bed, has already begun to write something on a piece of paper that he hands me with a big smile. Straddle legged, he is standing in front of me. I read with some effort, the note that states the following in faulty German:

'Meine Name ist Karl Frey. Ich bin ein sehr bescheiden Mann, ich bin auch gelehrte Mann. Ich sprechen english, französisch, italiënisch und nicht gut deutsch. Ich bin student an Hochschule in Chicago. Ich bin gekommen um zu machen alle Nazi kaput. Wenn du brauchen Hilfe, haben Angst, ich will helfen Du, und sehr gut, Good luck, K. Frey' [1]

---

[1] "My name is Karl Frey. I am a very modest man (but) I am also an educated man. I speak English, French, Italian, and not very good German. I am high school student in Chicago. I came here to eliminate all the Nazis. When you need help or you are afraid, I will help you and (I will do it) well. Good luck. K. Frey."

He is still standing in front of me with widely spread legs, while inside the tent the loud sound of the accordion is to be heard. He stretches out his big strong hand and taps me on the shoulder reassuringly. I can go! I am off as fast as I can go. The many years of imprisonment have made me quite shy, especially when five men cross my path!

So during the days that remain, before we are able to get back home, we can walk to our heart's content. On request, passes are handed out to let you go outside the camp but not for too long and different each time. In this way I get a permit that is valid from nine o'clock in the morning till three in the afternoon. Now, I have access to the area where before the liberation only a few prisoners ever had the opportunity to even glance. I am referring to the crematorium and its surroundings.

The crematorium was built in 1942 by priests. At the time, it was all done very secretly, for the name chosen for the labor *Kommando* (each *Kommando* carried a particular name) was such that it was never clear to outsiders that an oven was being constructed. It was namely called *Bau Kommando Barracks X.* Before, a few small sheds stood on the place, each with an oven that was used for burning corpses. When that became insufficient, a new modern building was erected. Now, after liberation, I have the opportunity to draw some pencil sketches of it. When I arrive, a wall surrounds the entire area. My eye immediately falls on "Barracks X," the crematorium. Piles of over 2000 corpses are still there, not yet burnt—daily, more companions died than the ovens can manage. I can even see two female figures in the horrible heaps of dead comrades. The corpses are in an advanced state of decomposition. Their faces look green and black. It is terrible to see.

Like firewood, they lie piled up on top of each other, covered with lots of quicklime. Hundreds of flies, beetles, worms and other vermin are crawling around. The stench here is unimaginable and the wind is spreading it all over the camp. The odor of dead bodies is a heavy and sickly smell with a cloying sweetness. The mixture of decomposition and chloroform makes us sick and nauseated.

Now that I stand here, I realise just how many victims have fallen in the camp, especially during these final weeks. Added to that the fact that Dachau is only one of so many camps, only one station— how many of such concentration camps can be counted in all of Germany? More than anyone can suspect! How pointless and meaningless all that has ever been written, done or thought seems, when something like this appears to be possible. Everything is a lie and without any value, when a culture of thousands of years cannot prevent such killings from happening happen in the 20th century. I am struck by a trembling, deep grief and only one thought keeps going through my mind: "Why ever all this? Why?"

I move on and enter the building. Everywhere I can smell the same disgusting stench of burning. Here are four big ovens; they look like ovens in a bakery. In the beginning, one or, at the most, two corpses were shoved inside. However nowadays, since it is "high season," I count seven in two ovens, and in both of the others, even nine corpses have been pushed in. The light red flames crinkle around the corpses and so they are being consumed, slowly but surely. Using big hooks and tongs, the prisoners who work here keep lugging along more corpses, so that the oven is burning constantly.

In front of the ovens, I can see strong iron rings attached to a beam. Here the poor devils were hung, to become ashes in the sea of flames immediately afterwards. The crematorium is bound on both sides by morgues that are often packed to the roof with dead bodies. On the left hand side, you enter a front room through a small hallway. Here a sign above one of the doors says "Showers." In reality, it is a gas chamber. A profound feeling of tightening inside of me overwhelms me when I enter here. Showers are hanging from the ceiling. I see drains with grids. The steel door can be closed airtight. As soon as the condemned were inside, it was possible to finish off many men within a short period of time by opening the gas supply. Out of the showers, gas came instead of water! I cannot say anything about the number of people that have been gassed here.

Outside again, behind the building, I see a shooting area, screened of by mats of rush. Here, those condemned to death were to kneel at a small hill, to be finished off by a shot in the back of the neck. A bit further on is the place where mass executions were carried out. Here on this spot, many people, mainly Russians, were murdered.

I pray and move my lips in a silent prayer for all those who have fallen as victims of the Nazi regime. Then I return to the camp.

Approximately eight days, in which we are not to leave the camp, pass. Yet, the desire to leave the camp once and for all keeps on burning. Every nationality chooses a trusted representative, who talks over the possibilities of returning home with the American commander. Rumors of how and when all this will happen go around. Some countries have their own news bulletin, with all the latest camp news.

The Dutch colony has its own news agency too, in the form of a daily newspaper "Voice of the Low Lands." The well-known Dutch writer Ed Hoorni belongs to the editorial staff.

On Wednesday, May 2, 1945, the first edition comes out. The opening article of the editorial board begins as follows, "Dutch people in Dachau, we are free. Our words need no longer be whispered; they can be spoken, sung and printed too in the open."

"Voice of the Low Lands," number 9, May 10, 1945, opens with the following message, "Not by order of any official authority but from their own initiative – which deserves words of honor and thanks – after a two days journey, the Dutch chaplains, Schellekens and Van Helden, chaplains in the Dutch underground army, in the company of Private Van der Krabbe have arrived in Dachau today by car, all the way from Nijmegen." On their return to the Netherlands, they will take Willem Boellaard and Deacon Teulings to help organise repatriation to the Netherlands.

After a while, the Dutch group gets permission to change their living quarter in the camp to a larger garage outside the camp, where they can wait for the final return to the Netherlands. This is quite an improvement, because like I said, overpopulation in the camp is such that many still have to sleep on the floor. Now, each of us gets a straw-mattress of his own, and in the big hall are plenty of beds, so that one gets a good night's sleep in the end. Other groups have been assigned a new "home" in former SS buildings in the area around the camp.

Day after day goes by, until finally on the Saturday before Pentecost, there are incredible cheers from our group. Dutch soldiers, even including a priest in uniform, have arrived by truck. They tell us that they were sent ahead to organise everything and that a train will arrive soon to bring us to the Netherlands. The next day, their truck will leave, taking with them twenty men.

"Voice of the Low Lands" number 16, May 19, 1945: "This afternoon, Chaplain Van Helden, Private Van der Krabbe, and two assistants have arrived by truck from the Netherlands. The first two are well known to us. They left for the Netherlands on May 12 in the company of our trusted representative, W. Boellaard, and the Deacon of Nijmegen. … The truck that will return to the Netherlands tomorrow will carry the following of our comrades…." A list with names is printed and, at number ten, I read my name: B. Tijhuis, Rijssen.

Who can describe my joy and surprise, when late in the evening, I hear that I am one of the first lucky ones who will leave the next morning. I can hardly believe it, because I am convinced that the elderly and those with family and children will go before me. It is agreed, however, that those with the longest "time" will be the first to greet freedom. I am such a privileged person with my five years of imprisonment, and so, with a lot of disbelief, I really see my name on the list hanging on the door. My joy is limitless and I hasten to pack the few belongings that I want to bring back with me.

The next morning, at seven, we leave. In the early morning, another three confreres celebrate Mass before they get onto the truck. Each of us gets a food parcel for the trip. After much handshaking, congratulations and farewells, we are off. The truck is decorated with a huge red-white-and-blue flag. With a heartfelt "See you in the Netherlands" we drive off. The American guard opens the gate with a merry face. Once again, we look over our shoulder to the place where we had to stand several years of torture and pain and learned what it means to be hungry and thirsty. A fervent *Deo Gratias,* more fervent than ever, comes over my lips now that it is all over … and, at full speed, we take off in the direction of our homeland!

APPENDIX A
DACHAU CONCENTRATION CAMP

On March 21, 1933, the daily newspaper *München-er Neueste Nachrichten* published a communiqué signed by Heinrich Himmler, future head of the SS "On Wednesday, March 22, the first concentration camp, accommodating 5,000 people will be inaugurat-ed in the neighborhood of Dachau."

The first inhabitants of the camp were political pris-oners: communists, social-democrats, all those consid-ered or suspected of being hostile to the Nazi regime and antifascists. They worked very hard to turn the place, an old ammunition factory, into a "rehabilita-tion camp," as the Nazis described the place. In fact, these prisoners had to build their own prison. Later on, a significant part of the political prisoners were all those deported – on the basis of the *Nacht und Nebel* decree (Night and Fog) – who were accused or suspect-ed of being enemies of the Third Reich.

The next group of prisoners to arrive were criminals mainly belonging to two sub-groups. Some had al-ready been in jail for their crimes but were nevertheless seen as unreliable persons, and were therefore interned in concentration camps. Other, while serving sen-tences of 5, 10, 20 years or even life sentences, were taken out of jail and sent to a concentration camp. The most merciless members of the camp's staff – *Blockäl-testen* and Kapo's – were recruited from among them. The SS referred to them as *Kommunisten*, an insult go-ing back to the early days when Communists were the first camp inmates. (Whenever Raphael is writing about "Communists," he is referring to either a Kapo in his block or in a labor work group).

In December 1940, Germany counted a large number of concentration camps and smaller labor camps, when an order came from Berlin to send all the imprisoned priests and other clergy to Dachau. The priests were assigned to two barracks, Numbers 26 and 28, and separated from the camp's other prisoners. Barracks 30 was reserved for only Polish priests. In Poland, the Catholic Church was severely hit by the Nazis. By 1939, a large percentage of the Catholic clergy and five bishops had been deported to concentration camps.

Dachau is a paradox among the Nazi concentration camps. It was Calvary for at least 2,600 Catholic priests from 24 nations. Yet it was also the only concentration camp to have a Catholic chapel where Mass was celebrated regularly. At first, this was a privilege granted only to the German priests in Barracks 26. By the end of 1942, however, all priests were allowed to attend mass.

For five years, *Konzentrationslager* Dachau, a small spot in the moors northwest of Munich, was the site of the largest religious community in the world.

APPENDIX B
THE LANGUAGE OF THE CAMPS*

The concentration camp, as a world human destruction set apart, had its own language. Being a true *empire of death,* the language used was inevitably a *language of death.* The words in the list below are some of the main words used in the camps by the SS or inmates. Many of the words are brutal or rude slang. All names, inscriptions and orders by SS officers and camp staff meant – either overtly or in a cynical disguise – suffering, torture, blood and death.

Ab! – Move! Order usually accompanied by a kick of the boot or a blow with the fist.

Abort – Latrines

Abrücken! – To leave

Achtung! – Stand at attention, attention!

Antreten! – To fall into line (for roll-call, a control or a punishment)

Appelplatz – Roll-call square. Often it was the place where punished inmates were beaten or executed.

Arbeit macht frei – "Work makes one free," a sentence written in iron letters above the entrance gate of the camp.

Arbeitskommando – Work team.

Baumhangen – Punishment where prisoners were hanged from a pole by their hands twisted behind the back.

---

* from: http://www.jewishgen.org and http://www.isurvived.org

Bettenbau – A tortuous way to make the bed following very strict rules.

Bibelforscher – Member of the Jehovah Witness religion.

Bock – Torture block. A prisoner had to lean over it to "receive" 25 or more strikes from a whip or club on his back and upper legs.

Block – Barracks

Blockälteste – Barracks chief, an elderly inmate of the barrack, most of the time a criminal.

Blockführer – SS in charge of a barracks.

Blöde Hund – Stupid dog (SS insult)

Brotzeit – Bread distribution

B.V. – Abbreviation for "Berufsverbrecher", criminal.

Dreck – Shit, dunghill. A word, used by the SS in a lot of insults, e.g. "Dreckhund," "Dreckjude," etc.

Durch Kamin – "Through the chimney" (of the crematorium) – an expression used by the SS for inmates who were in a terminal stage of weakness.

Effektenkammer – Room where the personal belongings of the inmates were stored.

Entlausungskommando – Work team in charge of delousing other inmates.

Flucht – Escape. The SS often used the expression "auf der Flucht erschossen" (killed during an attempted escape), when they shot an inmate during work.

Fluchtverdächtig – Prisoner suspected of escaping.

Fünf-und-zwanzig – 25 knocks with a club. One of the most common punishments in the camps.

Grüne – Green. A prisoner wearing a green triangle, meaning he was a professional criminal. They were often in charge of the most important functions in the camps. Most of the time, these prisoners were sadists and perverts.

Gummi – Club

Häftling – Inmate; detainee in a Nazi concentration camp, having no rights and not being protected by any law or international convention.

Haupttor – Main entrance of the camp

Himmelfahrtkommando – Literally "Ascension Commando." In Dachau, it was the team in charge of the non-exploded bombs. Very few of them survived. Also used for a transport composed of prisoners who were to be gassed.

Himmelkreuz und Wolkenbruch – SS insult.

Hinleggen – To fall on the ground during "exercises" invented by the SS. The inmates had to fall on the ground, then stand up and jump, again and again for hours at a time. Any inmate who was too weak to continue was immediately executed.

Hocker – Small wooden stool used inside the barracks, often used by the SS for the hangings.

Holzschuhe Wooden shoe. These shoes were a real nightmare for the inmates. After a few days, the feet were injured and bleeding. To be injured meant you were not able to work so the risk of being executed or sent on a transport to the gas chamber was great.

Hüpfen – To jump. This was another punishment "exercise" invented by the SS.

Hurra, hurra, ich bin wieder da! – "Hurray, hurray, I'm back again!" Inmates who had tried to escape and were later recaptured by the SS had to wear a board with these words written on it. They were always tortured, then usually hanged.

Invalide – Invalid
Invalidentrasport – Convoy sent directly to the gas chamber.

Jourhaus – Guard tower and office at the entry of the camp.
Jude – Jew
Judebrut – SS insult

Kapo – An inmate wearing a black band on the left arm on which *KAPO* was written in Gothic letters. A *Kapo* could be chief over a labor group or a maintenance team in the camp; he could accompany the marching columns or maintain order in the *Appellplatz*. He could strike, beat or kill any prisoner who did not belong to the inner hierarchy of the camp. Most of the time, he was a professional criminal, ready to do anything in order to keep his position in the hierarchy of the camp. Kapos were the ones who, faced with the alternative to die or to kill, preferred to kill. In order to prove their servility and to maintain their position as chiefs, they tried to surpass the SS in ferocity and cruelty.
Kartoffeln – Potatoes
Kommando – Work team
Kommandoführer – SS officer in charge of a work team.
Kommando X – Inmates who were working in the crematories in Dachau.
Kommunist – Communist (SS insult)
Kost – Food

Kostträger – Inmate in charge of bringing food to the barrack.

Krematorium – Crematorium.

Kretiner – Idiot (SS insult)

Kübel – Soup or coffee kettle

Kübelträger – Inmates who had to carry the heavy kettle.

Küche – Kitchen

K.Z. or **K.L.** – Abbreviation for *Konzentrationslager*, concentration camp.

Lager – Camp

Lagerälteste – Inmate, most often a criminal, who was responsible for the discipline in the camp.

Lagerarzt – SS doctor of the camp. They often executed inmates by lethal injections.

Lagerfürher – SS officer in charge of the camp.

Lagerkommandant – SS officer, commander of the camp.

Lagerpolizei – Police of the camp composed by inmates. They were hated by the other inmates.

Lagerprominent – An inmate who had a good job.

Lagerschreiber – Inmate working on an administrative job in the camp.

Lagerstrasse – Main street of the camp.

Lauseweg – "Louse street." Russian and Polish inmates had a large line shaved on their head, from forehead to neck. This line was called "louse street."

Lauskontrolle – Louse inspection. In several camps, an inmate having lice was immediately executed. The common expression was "Ein Laus, dein Todt" (one louse, your death).

Leichenkommando – Work team in charge of the corpses.

Mist – dunghill, a word used as an insult by the SS, like in "Mistjude."

Mittagstunde – Midday break time. Some bread was distributed during this break.

Moor-express – Wagon used for the transport of corpses to the crematory in Dachau.

Muselmann – Muslim. This expression was used for inmates who were too weak for work. The "muslims" died very fast.

Mütze – Cap

Mütze ab/Mütze auf – Cap on/cap off. An order given by the SS. When an inmate had to talk to an SS member, he had to remove his cap first.

N.N. – Abbreviation for "Nacht und Nebel" (Night and Fog). This was a special status for political prisoners. Nobody knew where they were and their families had no news from them. They just vanished into the "night and fog."

Ochsenschwanzsuppe – Oxtail soup. This was ironically used to designate the "soup" served to the inmates, most of the time just warm water with some rotten vegetables floating in it.

Organisieren – To steal from the SS.

Pfaffen – SS insult used for priests or clergy from all religions.

Pfleger – Male nurse

Polak – Polish. (SS insult)

Polnischer Urlaub – "Polish Vacation" – SS expression used for an inmate who had escaped.

Premiënschein – "Good for a prize." Each time an SS killed an inmate, he was receiving a prize or some days off.

Prügel – Knocks

Quarantaine – Quarantine. New inmates were placed in quarantine during some weeks.

Revier – Infirmary. The infirmary was always a very dangerous place to be, since ill inmates were often sent directly to the gas chamber or given a lethal injection.

Rot – Red. A political prisoner wearing a red triangle (communist).

Rollen – To roll on the ground. An SS "exercise" forced on prisoners.

Rollwagen – Wagon.

Rühet euch! – Quiet!

Russe – Russian (SS insult)

Sakrament, sakramenthund – priest (SS Insult)

Saupfaff – priest (SS Insult)

Scheisserei – Diarrhea due to starvation or dysentery. It was very common in the camps and one of the main causes of death.

Scheisskommando – Work team in charge of cleaning the bathrooms. Being assigned to this work was a punishment.

Schonung – Inmates who did not have to work.

Schreiber – Secretary.

Sicherheitsdienst – a special security unit of the SS.

Singen! – Sing! Order given by the SS during work.

Sonderkost – Special food for ill inmates. Everybody talked about it but nobody had ever seen it.

Still stehen – To stand still. A punishment; an inmate was forced to stand still for hours until he fell on the ground. Then he was shot.

Stink – To stink. (SS insult)
Strafkompagnie – Punishment company.
Stube – Chamber.
Stube-älteste – Inmate in charge of a room.
Stube-dienst – Inmate in charge of the cleaning of a
room.

Verbrecher – Inmate wearing a green triangle, sign of a
criminal.
Versuchskaninchen – Prisoner used for medical experiments.

Zimmerdienst – Inmates in charge of the rooms.
Zugangblock – Barracks where newly arrived prisoners had to wait until they were assigned to a work
team.

APPENDIX C
RETROSPECT:
"HEAVEN IS APPROACHING US"

With a fair sense of humor and a great deal of cleverness Raphael Tijhuis (1913-1981) manages to survive five years of imprisonment, three of which are in the concentration camp of Dachau. From the age of twenty-six until he is thirty-one he is locked up and has to endure inhuman torments. No doubt, apart from being young, he is very strong, both physically as well as mentally. Yet these years will leave significant marks on his future life. He seldom talks about it, but concentration camp syndrome is the cause of an increasing psychological disintegration. The hunger of Dachau keeps on haunting him every day, making him into a compulsive eater. He becomes overweight and has heart-trouble as a consequence. Cautious attempts to make him stick to the prescribed diet are parried with indignation: "You have no idea at all what it is like to be hungry!" When the American prior of his monastery in Rome comes to visit him at the hospital, he reacts to him as if he were an SS officer. In the end, his being a Dachau survivor, hunger and fear, engraved in his mind by numerous horrors, caused his premature death in 1981.

It seems a tragedy that he did not live to attend the beatification of Titus Brandsma in 1985, but it is certain that during the month they spent together in Dachau, Brandsma came to be his spiritual companion. Not the only one for sure, for – spoken or unspo-

ken – many a conversation or gesture turns into spiritual guidance in this enormous school of spirituality:
people who have to live in the utmost nakedness and
hardship, but joined together to form a community in
which the light of Heaven becomes visible. Titus
Brandsma is a mentor to Raphael who helps him become conscious of the spiritual meaning of what he
sees and to discover the hand of God in this horrific reality. His writings about those five years of imprisonment, in circumstances unworthy of a human being,
describe an inner journey that also helps us to discover
that our actual situation leaves a space for the Hidden
One. Normally we consider the superficial reality (especially in terrible circumstances) in an obsessive way,
so that we miss the insight that even here we find a
mystical space of God's presence. Evil never has the final word when we keep our eyes upon the hidden Face
of God's loving presence. Indeed, as Raphael writes
clearly, "The devil is in charge, but Heaven is with us."
These years have thus made him into a truly contem-
plative Carmelite, standing ceaselessly before God's
face. That is why he remains faithful to the numerous
confreres and their experience that God is present to
them, even in the hell of Dachau. He has to speak
about it in the name of those who have died.

This book is a relevant part of war documentation,
since it outlines an aspect that is easily forgotten. War
is not just caused by violence and hatred and the rightful opposition against them, but above all is a consequence of people's failure to grant each other the God-
given room to live. The story of Raphael Tijhuis is one
of those stories that document how people respond to
aggression and the negation of their validity by search-
ing for the very essence of human existence. Sure, a de-

cent society and a brotherhood of humanity require the liberation from occupying and oppressive forces, but the most fundamental answer to aggression might be found in the spiritual journey of those people who dare to listen to the Word of God in all circumstances.

However necessary a condition of being liberated from occupying forces and oppressive powers may be for a society, worthy of humanity and humane brotherhood, the most fundamental answer is to be found in the spiritual journey of people who dare to listen to God's address in all circumstances.

Raphael does not know Titus Brandsma intimately before they meet in Dachau during a phase in their spiritual journey, which is of crucial importance to both of them. To Raphael this encounter means a confirmation of spiritual intuitions he was brought up with and had gathered in his formative years as a young Carmelite. In Titus' attitude he sees that love is stronger than death and destruction. He has probably never heard or read Titus' words in his sermon on peace in the Bergchurch at Deventer in 1931,[1] but he can see now what these words mean in practice.

> Everyone strives after his own interest, harder still for his own possessions, and there appears to be no way of solving the conflicting interests in the dispute of each for his own. The way of the world is such that if one does not resist, he will be trampled underfoot, and

---

[1] Cf. Hein Blommestijn, Blessed Titus Brandsma (1881-1942), Prophet of Peace – Martyr of Dachau, in: *The Canadian Catholic Review*, vol. 4, 1986, no 4, 19/139-25/145. Titus Brandsma – Prophet of Peace and Martyr of War, in: *Carmel in the World* (Rome) 25, 1986, n. 1, 21-33. Titus Brandsma – Vredesprofeet en oorlogsmartelaar, in *Speling* 36, 1984, nr. 4, 42-49.

only resistance can advance a person. It is thought, nay, openly proclaimed, that principles of peace and love are unavailing in society, that one must be strong in the struggle for existence and must make oneself ever stronger, because the might of the strongest makes right.[2] Selfishness and greed are the great evils of these times and the deepest causes of war. We must make a stand against these. Only then can we work effectively for peace.[3]

Brandsma understands the logic of war better than anyone, but lacks the skill to escape sharp blows. To him the inhumanity of the Nazi system remains unimaginable. While Titus has little chance to survive the hell of Dachau due to poor health, Raphael remains upright. With his humor and cleverness, he creates the spiritual room in which he never ceases to be mindful of the Hidden One. Having an excellent psychological insight, he sees through the logic of power and tries to escape blows if possible and even to improve his position. Sound self-interest and loving brotherhood help him to build a community where life is possible despite everything. More and more, he discovers the blessings of prayer and the Eucharist. He loves to draw on traditional forms of prayer like the rosary and the Stations. He meditates on the "greatest Prisoner and Sufferer of all times" and finds the strength to persevere in this abyss of anguish and terror. Thus he is able to see a reality that is more essential—"Heaven is approaching us."

---

[2] *Mystiek leven. Een bloemlezing*, serie Spiritualiteit, dl. 21, Nijmegen 1984, 163. Transl. Joachim Smet.
[3] *Idem*, 168.

As he describes events and untold suffering, we recognise a spiritual growth that is bringing him closer and closer to his religious calling. He could recognise this growth in the men around him as well, and he has to speak of it, now that his deceased confreres have entered into the eternal silence of God's unconditional love for ever. A spiritual journey is difficult to put into words, for it is not until he is in Dachau that Raphael really is to discover the solitude of Carmel:

> For a long time I have thought about whether I would write about Dachau or keep silent. Why talk about it? People would not be able to understand at all; I no longer belong to the others and other people no longer belong to me.

Sure enough, what's the use of telling others about something when there are no words? Speaking about our relation to God is easily frustrated by disbelief and scepticism of "realists." This is an insight Raphael shares with Titus, a professor in the history of Dutch mysticism, not afraid of writing about experiences of being touched by God in a column in the *Gelderlander*, a regional newspaper. Why keep silent about the incredible approach of the Beloved?

> If we cannot find around us an understanding of the true concept of a peace rooted in society, then something is lacking in people's receptivity to that concept, then opposition to war is not what is needed, then we must look deeper, then ailing society must be reformed.
> When that sickness threatens soon to become again total madness, then it is time that we as quickly as possible devise a way to arrest that sickness in its growth

and to irradiate that spreading cancer with the rays of our healthy understanding and thus put an end to its destructive work.[4]

That is the reason why we have to speak about Love. It is the only way out of the terror of war. Titus Brandsma fought for exactly this peace in his own natural way. His actual involvement with social and political problems of his times and his study of mysticism are not two separate worlds that have nothing to do with each other. One cannot live without the other. As a prophet of peace he is an apostle of love as well. During the national pilgrimage to Dokkum in 1939 his words in a sermon at Leeuwarden are as follows:

We live in a world in which even love is condemned and spoken of as a weakness that we have to get rid of, that has to be overcome. "No more love but self-empowerment"; "Let each person become as strong as possible, let the weak go down." Christianity with its preaching of love is supposed to be out of time and needs to be replaced by ancient Germanic force! Oh yes, they come to you with those dogmas and there are people who are very receptive to it. Love is in denial; *Amor non amatur*, is what St. Frances of Assisi said; and a couple of centuries later St. Magdalena de Pazzi rang the bells of the Carmelite nunnery in ecstasy to let people know how wonderful love is. Oh, how I would love to make bells ring to tell the world how wonderful love is. Now that neo-paganism has abolished love, we will – mindful of history – conquer that same heathenness through love and not abandon our love. Love will make us regain the hearts of the pagans. Nature over-

---

[4] *Idem*, 166-167.

comes dogma. Never mind if theory dismisses and condemns love and labels her a weakness, The practice of life will always make her into a strength that will conquer and capture the hearts of people. "See how they love each other." These are words, spoken by the first Christians, which the neo-pagans have to be able to say about us anew. Thus we will conquer the world.[5]

This is not just a "sermon." Titus Brandsma remains faithful till the bitter end, as Raphael, as an eyewitness, tells us. It is as if Titus finds his true greatness in these conditions of merciless destruction. He never panics. He is not taken over by anxiety to save his own skin. Prison and concentration camp are the very places where he enjoys the quiet and silence of the mystical experience that he has longed for all his life. To his surprise, this is what Raphael discovers too. That is why he makes himself into a messenger of the "plain truth." For, in his words, in Dachau he has "learned to value people and things more than before."

> To have found the way to deepen one's inner life and to be a Christian means so much more. This would mean victory over the shadow of evil and the devilish forces of the dark, which we encountered there.

Like Titus Brandsma, Raphael knows that the essence is only to be found when we embrace Love and relate to each other from that same Love. By doing so, we enter into a different world, a world not made by human hands.

---

[5] *Idem*, 191-192.

> When I consider my time in the concentration camp
> and three prisons in the light of faith, not a single sparkle
> of hatred or any feeling of revenge enters my heart. To a
> Christian, one thing has to be clear: above and beyond
> the feeling of human retaliation stands the law of love. I
> would strain the Lord's prayer, I would betray being a
> Christian, if I would not practice love of neighbor and
> forgiveness to all, without regard to political affiliation,
> religion or nationality, especially right now after every-
> thing that has happened.

During a period of five years, Raphael meditates on
the absurdity of an imprisonment that lacks any legal
basis. Looking back, he acknowledges that it has been
an irreplaceable school of Love to him and many of his
colleagues. Because he is dragged down into the dark
deep of the insanity of self-interest and discovers its insane and pointless character in his reflections, he opens
himself without hesitating to the Love that knows no
why. He takes his first step in this spiritual development
in the prison cell in Mainz, where its "desolate impression," is in such contrast to the "atmosphere of peace
and happiness" of his cloister cell.

> I kneel down and pray to Mary for help. She will be
> my strength in these dark days and the many more dark
> days to come. "Holy Mary, Mother of Mount Carmel,
> pray for us!" Then it is as if my cell turns into Heaven.
> The atmosphere of sadness is gone to make room for
> contentment and complete surrender to God's holy will.
> No threatening by any guard can scare me. Nobody is
> able to take away my peace.

By creating an inner space for the Hidden One, his
perspective on reality is changing. He refuses to give

up Sunday's rest. When the guard turns against him pale with rage, his insubordination is punished with unemployment. Raphael's reaction is quite down to earth and calm: "What else could I do than take my rosary again? I am much better at that." At the end of 1940, the thought of the suffering Christ becomes his "favorite meditation subject" in the prison of Pre-ungesheim. He knows that he is only a beginner on this impassable route.

> The principle motivation that I keep my eyes set on is the thought of the suffering Christ. The scene in which the tyrants mock Jesus is my favourite subject matter during meditation. I also like to let the story from the Mount of Olives, where Jesus speaks the *fiat* to his Father in Heaven, pass through my mind. In this situation I still feel so small, and I try to say my *fiat* and accept everything that is happening to me as coming from the hand of the Lord. After that I can carry on despite all the crosses that are bound to come.
>
> Not a day passes without praying the Stations, and only by doing this over and over again one grows to love and value them more and more. That is how I spend most of my time as soon as I return from work, also sometimes by praying my Office. After supper I take a book and read for a while until the light is switched off. Then I do my evening prayers and lay myself to rest.

Physically and mentally, he is inside a prison but inwardly he becomes more and more settled in his cloister cell. In his profession of the Carmelite rule he spoke his *fiat* unconditionally, as did Mary; it is his "yes" to God calling him. At that moment he does not know what this will bring to him. In accordance with the mystical tradition of Carmel, he will have to go where there is no road, to "accept whatever will happen out of the hand of the heavenly Father." This road knows no escapes, even when humanly speaking the burden becomes too hard to bear, and at the cost of his own life.

I decide that accepting my fate is much better than trying to escape. I surrender to God's Holy Will. Turning the loss of freedom, the greatest good mankind has, into an offering must be pleasing to the good Lord, I am sure. So I make it into a habit, almost second nature, to do a short act of surrender to the good Lord in my mind, or simply, a quick prayer like "Everything for You, my Jesus," each time the clock in the prison tower announces a new quarter hour. This I can do without anyone noticing.

In this way he prepares himself, without being aware of it, for the final refusal of the great seduction to say "yes" to the cowardly offer to save his skin by handing over his habit. He is able to see through these devilish tactics. Together with Elijah, the prophet, he remains upright, standing face to face with God without faltering.

"Well, tell your boss that under such conditions, I would rather go to Dachau and that I stand by my signature!" The other cell inmates, although none of them is a Catholic, think it is an extraordinary piece of Gestapo technique to attack a person at his deepest convictions in a moment when he is about to encounter the horrible monster "death" that lies in wait in the concentration camp. I take my rosary and pray to heaven for the mercy of assistance and strength in all the difficulties and dangers yet to be sustained and conquered.

Death in Dachau stalks mercilessly each day. To survive is hardly an option. The SS know very well that insecurity breaks resistance. Any perspective of time disappears in an endless waiting for nothing. Many hours and sometimes entire days at the roll-call square are transformed into a spiritual room where also prayer knows no limitations or bounds anymore. On the walls of this unthinkable "chapel", images of God's endless Love appear.

In general, the clergy use this time of waiting in the fresh early hour of the morning for a short and ardent prayer. This is the only time in the day when you have a few minutes to peacefully direct your thoughts to Him who is the Father of all and who does not forget us, even in the severest and most difficult times. A short meditation or a decade of the rosary, prayed in silence, fill the few minutes before the beginning of roll call. Then Heaven is besieged with prayers for strength from the good Lord for the new day.

While we stand there, we are often struck by the splendid colours of the rising sun. The horizon glows in the most divergent shades of golden yellow and vermilion, which then turn into a deep purple, and a glorious ultramarine. Those incredibly beautiful morning skies often catch the attention of all of us there. I do not think any painter has enough colours on his palette to be able to reproduce such a prodigy of nature with his brush. Such a sublime spectacle of nature can direct your thoughts for a few moments towards Him, the Creator of the universe, whose power and majesty knows no bounds.

Thousands of men are gathered in this enormous "chapel," celebrating a public worship of which the SS is totally ignorant. Psychological insecurity keeps their eyes focused on the Hidden One who forms their deepest essence. Thus, they acquire an intangibility and holiness, which disarm the SS and leaves them without power. In the silence and solitude of this sacred space they prepare in communion for the encounter with God.

> Titus often speaks of the "Great Prisoner" Christ in the Blessed Sacrament. He points out to me how Christ Himself has been a prisoner and how he has endured so much mockery and derision, flagellation, the crowning with thorns and crucifixion simply out of love for us, and that we have to bear our imprisonment for love of Him. "Above all, let's not forget this, whenever something painful happens to us here. We have to use that moment to respond to his love. How trivial is everything that we experience here in comparison with what he has suffered for us," he tells me.

So all the time, imprisonment and martyrdom acquire totally different meanings. Unnoticed, physical destruction turns into mystical "nonbeing" that frees them from self-concern and subtle self-reflection. Because they contemplate that "what they have to go through here is little compared to what He has endured for us," they are transformed into God's unconditional Love. Darkness turns into an overwhelming light, as their imprisonment is the road to freedom at the same time. Raphael remembers very clearly the words of Titus Brandsma who precedes him in this. "Dear Friend, Dachau with all its difficulties and perils is like a dark tunnel through which we have to pass. We must hold on and keep courage. At the end, the

eternal Light that will set us free, is shining." As a survivor of Dachau, he knows that the liberation of 1945
is only relative, and does not mean that much as long
as we do not enter into the abode of the Hidden One
who is our true Life.

At the end of 1942, medical experiments that he has
to undergo bring Raphael to the edge of death. He
longs to be chosen, like his friends Titus Brandsma and
Henny Zwaans, to reach the end of the "dark tunnel"
and to become part of eternal glory.

> I do not care if I live or if I die now, I am prepared
> for anything. It would mean redemption, if the good
> Lord would come and take me during these dire times.
> Yet I want to be cured. Energy and the young life are
> really struggling indeed. I wait patiently, entirely sur-
> rendered to God's will, praying as far as praying is pos-
> sible, because I often lack the strength. Good inten-
> tions, however, even turn the smallest word into a
> God-pleasing prayer, so throughout all the pain, I can
> only hope to live and do something good.

While his body has a fever of 40.6 C and he is fighting to survive, everything becomes a silent prayer. Even
in his failure to pray properly he experiences God's ex-
tended hand that leads us into his Love. Christmas 1942
at the malaria ward in the *Revier* – his first Christmas in
Dachau but the third one as a prisoner – is an experience of intense religious intimacy to Raphael. The utter
forsakenness, experienced at the same time, makes a
stinging contrast: "The terrible forlornness that weighs
on me, reminds me more than ever of the great Forsakenness of the Savior." Good Friday and Christmas
are holding out hands to each other.

Sitting at the edge of my straw mattress, I listen to the gentle Polish Christmas Carols. Their tender melodies are gratifying to my heart and soul, so that we almost forget about the miserable concentration camp. Warm tears that we are not ashamed of at all, run down our hollow cheeks. We understand that as much as joy had been present in the stable, the same could happen in a camp as long as Christ is among us. Christ lives in our hearts, because a good friend of mine has brought us Holy Communion despite the great dangers that come with it. I will never forget those days!

His report on the final two years in Dachau becomes less focused on events. More and more Raphael becomes a keen observer, and he pictures the system where so many of his friends found their last resting place. What started as a personal story of things that happened during five years of imprisonment, developing into a spiritual (auto) biography, ends almost like a spiritual treaty. To him, these years are not just a school of lived spirituality, but find meaning as a school of reflection as well.

Despite everything, there have been nice moments as well. The good moments in Dachau are all religious in character. You can see faithful Christians really live their faith. From the moment I arrived in the camp and my habit and everything else were taken from me, my ties with the past were broken but I felt more and more guided by God. He is the One with whom I feel connected in all circumstances. His omnipresence, a truth that once was not much more than theory, is an intense experience here and takes shape in a way that often feels benevolent. His providence is the pillow where we lay our tormented souls at rest. You know God will lead you. No matter what may happen, it only happens according to His will. In the absence of human satisfaction, one achieves the complete surrender to God's providence, and thus to God. Lack of everything that is needed to live creates more room for the Mysterious. I must confess that every now and then I look back to those difficult years with some feeling of nostalgia. Never have I felt closer to God. The electrified barbed wire could not prevent God from reaching us.

Unnoticed, while looking back on the impassable road, Raphael transforms into a spiritual companion of the reader. In this, he remains faithful to his calling to give a voice to the deceased who saw the Light in Dachau. We all have to go the way, as it is coming towards us unasked. Each one of us has to encounter death and make friends with her.[6] The God of Life will kiss us awake in utter silence and solitude. Beyond the beyond! There, we will become an open space where the Hidden One may reveal His presence.

Lauwersmeer, August 28, 2004.

Jos Huls and Hein Blommestijn

---

[6] Jos Huls, De dood als vriend – Dag Hammarskjöld, in *Speling* 53 (2001) 1, 74-81.

The Carmelite church and monastery on *Karmeliterstrasse* in Mainz, Germany as it appeared in 2007. It was here that Br. Raphael was arrested on July 25, 1940, by the Gestapo.

(Photo courtesy of the CITOC Photo Archives, Rome)

Three Carmelites, future victims of the Nazi terror, photographed together in the funeral procession for the Bishop of Mainz, Ludwig M. Hugo, on April 12, 1935. [Far left in white cloak] Fr. Titus Brandsma (who would later die in Dachau), [second from left in white cloak] Fr. Thaddäus Karpinski (who would die in December 1943 on the Eastern Front), and [first from right, partially hidden, in white cloak] Br. Raphael Tijhuis (who was arrested by the Gestapo on July 25, 1940, for comments he wrote in letters to his Dutch family and friends).
(Photo: Archives of the Lower German Carmelite Province)

Brother Raphael Tijhuis in the courtyard of the Carmelite monastery in Mainz before his arrest. Raphael was a member of the Dutch Province which was re-establishing the Lower German Province of Carmelites after its suppression during the Secularization of 1802. The Carmelites originally came to Mainz in the late 1200s. Fr. Titus Brandmsa, also a member of the Dutch Province, was very instrumental in the return of the Carmelites to Mainz.
(Photo: Archives of the Lower German Carmelite Province)

The former sacristy and now the community chapel in the Carmelite monastery in Mainz. It was here, as he assisted the prior of the monastery in preparing to celebrate Mass, that Br. Raphael learned that the Gestapo was waiting for him.

Christchurch in Mainz. From his prison cell in the early weeks of his confinement, Raphael could hear "the beautiful heavy bells of the nearby Christchurch chiming on Sunday" and "I even manage to catch the sound of our own bells resounding over the roofs of the town. I sink in a mood of melancholy and nostalgia ..."
(Photo courtesy of CITOC Photo Archives)

Carmelite Fr. Titus Brandsma (circa 1935). Most of his life was dedicated to scholarship and journalism. He gained renown throughout the Netherlands as a spiritual master, was one of the founders of the Catholic University of Nijmegen (now Radboud University), as well as an accomplished journalist. But it is for his relentless defense of the Dutch people and the Church against the Nazi hatred for which he is best remembered. This ultimately cost him his life. As part of Nijmegen's 2000th anniversary celebrations in 2005, its citizens voted Blessed Titus Brandsma as the "Greatest Citizen of Nijmegen Of All Time." He was beatified by Pope John Paul II in November 1985.
(Photo: NCI, Boxmeer)

(Detail) Polish Carmelite, Blessed Hilary Januszewski, as a student, in a community picture taken in the courtyard of *Collegio di Sant' Alberto* in Rome during a visit of the Cardinal Protector of the Order. Blessed Hilary and several other Polish Carmelites were interned in Dachau along with Blessed Titus Brandsma and Br. Raphael Tijhuis, both from the Netherlands. A residence with a theology faculty for Carmelite students from around the world, *Sant' Alberto* also was home to Titus Brandsma when he was a student and to Br. Raphael Tijhuis following his release from Dachau.
(Photo: General Archives of the Carmelite Order, Rome)

The Carmelite monastery in Krakow, Poland where Fr. Hilary Januszewski was prior. Today the church continues to draw people devoted to *Our Lady on the Sands*, a devotion dating back to the 1300s.
(Photo: Polish Province)

A memorial to Blessed Hilary Januszewski, former prior, in the courtyard of the monastery in Krakow, Poland. Fr. Hilary was arrested on December 4, 1940, at the Krakow monastery when he attempted to help Carmelites the Gestapo had come to arrest. At Dachau, Bl. Hilary volunteered to assist with the care of inmates suffering from typhoid. He died just 21 days later, on March 26, 1945, at the age of 38 years, just one month before the American army liberated the concentration camp. He was beatified by Pope John Paul II on June 13, 1999. *(Photo: CITOC Photo Archives, Rome)*

The main gate to the Dachau concentration camp with the Nazi slogan "Work Brings Freedom." It is estimated that more than 200,000 prisoners from 30 countries passed through this gate.
(Photo: CITOC Photo Archives, Rome)

Memorial to the Prisoners of Dachau who perished. In the background is a reconstructed model of the prisoners' barracks. *(Photo: CITOC Photo Archives, Rome)*

An aerial view of Dachau Concentration Camp (KZ-Gedenkstätte Dachau) - Established in 1933 on orders of SS Fuhrer Heinrich Himmler, the camp was originally built to hold 5,000 prisoners. Its first prisoners were political opponents of the regime, communists, social demo crats, trade unionists, and members of conservative and liberal political parties. Later new groups were deported to the camp, including Jews, homosexuals, gypsies, members of the Jehovah's Witness, and religious leaders.

The camp's commandant developed an organizational plan and rules which became the standard for all the Nazi concentration camps. The prisoners' camp was surrounded by various security facilities and a camp command area with administrative buildings and barracks for the dreaded Nazi SS. *(Photo: USHMM Photo Archives)*

A memorial containing the ashes of victims of the Nazi death camp in Dachau. The words "Never Again" in Hebrew, French, English, German, and Russian express the hope of the world after it awoke to the horror of these Nazi camps. Some 30,000 are recorded to have died in Dachau but thousands who were not registered died from starvation and disease. Others were shot, hanged, or killed by lethal injections or so-called medical experiments. Most bodies were disposed of in the crematorium at the rear of the camp.
(Photo: CITOC Photo Archives, Rome)

Brother Rafael's sketch of the Marian altar in front of Barracks 26, one of the priests' barracks, after the liberation of the Dachau concentration camp. Many of Rafael's drawings of life inside the camp, still exist.
(Photo: Carmelite Library of the Lower German Province of Carmelites)

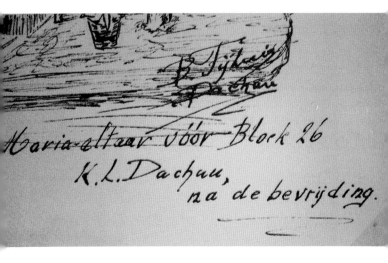

Brother Raphael's description of the sketch and his signature "B. Tÿhuis", using his baptismal name "Bernard" and an old form of writing the family name.
(Photo: Carmelite Library of the Lower German Province of Carmelites)

Brother Rafael Tijhuis a short time before his death on
June 5, 1981, in Mainz, Germany.
(Photo: Archives of the Lower German Carmelite Province)